Budd

Budding Thoughts

BY

Nancy Budd

www.bookstandpublishing.com

Published by
Bookstand Publishing
Morgan Hill, CA 95037
3481_3

ISBN 978-1-61863-049-0

Printed in the United States of America

`

<u>Acknowledgments</u>

It is truly amazing to me that this book has been completed. It could not have been accomplished without encouragement from my husband, Jerre, and my family who convinced me it could be done, and to all that have cheered me on and given helpful instructions.

My granddaughter, Mariah Budd, walked me through the intricacies of the Internet with extreme patience and enthusiasm, since the computer was not in my skilled area of accomplishment.

My granddaughter, Kate Stone, has given me permission to use her childhood likeness on the cover, for which I am very pleased.

The project has been completed with the Lord's blessing.

.

Table of Contents

Stories

Poems

Once in a while, something unique happens

Once in a while something unique happens in your private corner of the country that delights your soul and sparks you with hope and enthusiasm for life. It has happened to me, just two feet outside my kitchen window.

I'm an avid bird watcher; I tend my feeders faithfully year round. It probably has spoiled the feathered life in my neighborhood. They could find food in the summer, with a little more effort, while depending on the feeder system for the winter. But I like seeing and talking to them, while they chirp and chatter back to me. It is because of my year round tending that a family of finches, checking out real estate for a nesting sight, decided on my hanging bird feeder, to build their nest.

Refilling the feeder one day, I discovered several twigs and leaves in the feeder and quickly scooped them out, with the empty hulls of seed. The very next day there was a substantial amount of twigs and grass debris once again in the feeder. After observing a short while, the carrier was revealed. She was a very plain-feathered house finch.

More days passed. Momma finch, now nicknamed "Plain Jane", took up residency and within two days, one egg was nestled in the new home. I watched carefully from my kitchen window, moving slowly in that area so she wouldn't be disturbed. Each day a new egg was added until soon there were five in the nest.

Momma finch was in constant attendance unless startled away or feeding. Papa finch would sometimes visit on the edge of the nest and other times sit on the edge of the roof to observe and guard the nest.

Early on a Friday morning "Jane" had a visitor at her nest. Papa had come to admire the first of her brood, which hatched during the night. The baby hatchling, the tiniest fluff of feathers I had ever seen was fluttering in the nest.

Neighbors came to peer into the nest from inside my kitchen window. All were more than willing to use the front door to avoid disturbing the new parents who's nest was next to the back door. Our consensus counted a population of four chicks. Each day showed subtle changes. The feathers became larger and the babies grew larger and stronger.

After watching carefully for many days, I had to be away from my home for several days and when I returned I was surprised to find the nest empty. I observed discreetly for two more days and saw "Jane" return several times, perch on the edge a moment and fly away. Assuming the family had vacated, I removed the feeder, emptied and scrubbed it among many large swallows and cringing expressions on my face, then refilled it with fresh sunflower mix and rehung it.

Within two hours, two brightly colored young males and one young female were busily feeding in their cleaned ex-nest.

During the following month I was treated to early morning chirps and magnificent trills of song from my bird family as they confidently visited and ate their fill daily. Then one morning in early July, it was like déjà vu as I filled the feeder with seed and once again noticed bits of branch and twigs being gathered in the feeder.

Apparently my satisfied tenants are gracing our rental facilities for another term of family tending.

Not next year, not later, time to do it is now

The time to do it is now; not next year, not after you retire, not some day when you save up enough money – now!

Life has a way of rushing past us when we're not paying attention. Lifelong ambitions and dreams keep getting shoved back on the shelf waiting for a better time. Then suddenly, you are older, illness strikes, or "the someone special" to share the experience is taken from you. All of a sudden it's too late. Too late to wonder why you delayed that trip out west or maybe just a little up north or down south. Foolish reasons now, but so logical when you discussed them.

If a large plan isn't possible, scale it down to a reasonable size and reconsider. You can do it, at least sooner than you expected. It can be reducing a two-week trip to a long weekend to an interesting area of refreshment. Do you like the shore or mountains? Maybe you prefer an exciting weekend in the city to see a show and sightseeing. It doesn't matter where you go, just as long as you enjoy being there.

If time has already passed up some opportunities, think of another to take its place. Have you ever taken your son or grandson to a ballgame, or maybe an overnight camping session? A weekend in the city with a daughter or son to explore your special interests could be a memorable experience and a time to become better acquainted. They may get to know a side of you they never knew existed.

People that are enjoying life are the ones who are living it to the fullest measure. The good times can roll with you driving the cart or you can stand aside and watch them roll along without you. Don't let life and all its excitement pass you by -- do something now!

Whose watching who when it comes to 'models' these days?

Would you be comfortable if you knew someone else was trying to be just like you? Probably not. None of us are perfect.

At some time in our lives we all have lapses of good judgment or manners. The knowledge that someone observed our every action would be awesome and stressful enough to render us non-functional.

We can never be sure who selects us as a model to be copied. Perhaps it is one of our children, a neighbor's child, a co-worker, or if you are in public life, almost anyone observing you everyday.

You may be a foreman or manager at work in charge of other employees. Being Mr. Niceguy may make you well liked and a favorite of other employees, but being honest and fair in your treatment and attitude can also earn respect of our co-workers.

If you are a teacher, your responsibility to each student is of utmost importance. If you let students slide by without working up to their potential it may make you a favorite of some, but the student is going to remember the teacher who pushed gently and drew out the best he or she had to offer, however, not necessarily at the time it's being done. This process will also teach perseverance, study habits, and eventually excellence in their courses while instilling self-esteem.

You alone are responsible for the image you portray. You may be judged by your words or your attitude by people who may never have the opportunity to know you well. Those public observances may be the only occasion some people have to get to know anything about you.

Are people observing you as you encourage a friend or co-worker or try to understand another person's problems and offer help? Will they see you teach by example such important qualities as compassion, honesty and truthfulness?

Is your image a beacon to guide others or would you rather not be observed in your everyday living?

Think carefully about the impression that you leave for others. It may be the example others use to pattern their lives.

Not everybody is on the same schedule

How organized are you?

There are people who become rigid over a schedule, because it rattles them when they do not know what will happen next. Unless things go according to a plan, they find they are unable to function calmly.

As a nurse in an emergency room, a schedule only meant I was required to arrive at work on time and have everything ready for any emergency that might happen. Try to keep on a schedule with that format! It was a great training ground for motherhood.

As a mother, a schedule is always flex-time. A day that starts with promise can deteriorate rapidly with one sick child. Equally as disrupting is a stormy day when children are required to be in three different directions at almost the same time. It demands ingenuity and creativity when variables like children and weather enter the equation or scheduling. It is beneficial to acquire the capability of rolling with the changes.

Some people are persistent with their daily and weekly schedules and I admire them for this ability. It is an asset, for business people especially. Anyone able to control their time schedule can accomplish many more daily tasks than a person who has an unmanageable day.

I have not been able to perfect this skill in my own life. Certainly I managed to arrive on time for work and fulfill my duties on various levels of employment, but I guess I would extend my skills to other areas which required a more flexible timetable. I think that's called being sidctrackcd, but I functioncd morc happily on that level.

Today it is a popular trend to use a Daytimer for a scheduling tool. Try as I might, I can't seem to stick to the timetable. It seems like a happier and less hectic schedule for me to block out the major appointments, dentists, doctor, meetings, etc., and take the rest of the day as it comes. There are lots of interesting things to do in a day if you leave your options open.

Take time to do some of the things you like to do instead of always doing what you have to do. Some of the "have to do's" will still be able to be done tomorrow and in the meantime, you've done something special today.

How much lower can this society possibly sink?

Where are we headed in our country? How much farther will we descend? What will be the outcome of the downgrading of morals and lifestyles?

It is becoming difficult to distinguish what is 'not right' and what is 'normal'. So many types of behavior are considered to be 'normal' that they are accepted today as the proper thing to do.

Fifty percent or more of married couples end their marriages in divorce.

A large percentage of couples live together without marrying because that's what their friends are doing.

Many parents who grew up in the 60's actually expect their children to try or use drugs. I don't think they view it as a hazard because many did it themselves.

Our higher principles are not reinforced by many Hollywood movies, television shows and prominent people in the media that tend to glamorize drinking, drug taking and immoral sexual behavior. As these behaviors are glamorized, it seems to give acceptance and permission to our youth. It seems to say you will be popular and 'normal' if you live your life this way.

Young people newly graduated from college expect to start work at high salaries before they gain any business experience to warrant it. They think they are entitled to it because they went to college.

Young adults want now what their parents worked for and waited years before receiving. Many parents worked years as an apprentice before acquiring the job or position they desired.

Economy cars are looked down on in preference to a more expensive model or a van, because they want the vehicle with the better image. Station wagons are viewed as an old man's car and not as desirable, although they may be less expensive. Advertisers do their best to reinforce these ideas by convincing the viewer how important it is to make a good image through a particular model or product.

It seems to be much easier to get into serious debt today. Credit cards are so readily available with little mention of the high interest rates paid for using them. They actually discourage full payment monthly because it is more lucrative to the company. I've even read of credit card companies charging the customer for not using them enough. It is no wonder so many people are in financial difficulties or declaring bankruptcy.

Clothing fads and fashions seem to carry so much peer pressure that it is currently more popular to wear ragged, torn or deliberately sloppily oversized clothes in order to be in style. Some style. Are these the same people who didn't want to wear a sibling's hand-me-downs because they didn't fit right? Some of us may remember when it was nearly a disgrace to be seen wearing denim or overalls. It signified that your family was so poor that was all that could be afforded. Well, at least today that is no longer true. It requires quite a bit of money to buy denim clothing—at least the larger known brand names. They are now considered dress-up clothes.

Family unity is so fractured there does not seem to be a good example for a child to follow. Many, perhaps more than 50 percent of households are single parent homes. Childcare is very often outside the home and someone else may be teaching your child their family values instead of you. Who are your child's teacher, caretaker, disciplinarian, confidant and role model?

Fortunately everyone does not ascribe to this lifestyle. Many youth programs are gaining acceptance in schools and communities to encourage young people to refrain from drinking and using drugs. They are being told about and encouraged to enter a contract with their parents or church organization to save sex for marriage and uphold their moral values.

I hope these latter trends continue to flourish so that our children can be proud to be 'different' for not doing what is looked on as the popular behavior and turn our country and morality back to a higher standard to be emulated and looked upon as 'normal'.

Winter's not over yet; still time for snow to fall

What do you remember most about last winter?

Many conversations today seem to center around the weather. Even though it's been pretty cold lately, people are still complaining because they want to know where winter is. Winter meaning snow. To my memory, we had enough 'winter' last year to last for the next six years! There was more snow than I needed to see. On top of the snow there was ice and more ice to add to the misery, danger and added expense of dealing with the results or weather conditions.

If you owned a snow blower, perhaps you discovered it was inadequate to handle the extraordinarily large amounts of snow. If you had not estimated correctly the amount of ice-melt or sand you needed for your walks and driveway, you may have found it very difficult to locate any in the middle of the season.

Those who owned plows mounted on their vehicles found many opportunities to earn extra income plowing driveways and parking lots. If enough had not been budgeted for plowing, funds had to be shifted to meet the immediate expense. We even found it necessary to hire a front-end-loader to move the snow because we ran out of places to put it.

Many home-repairmen and handymen have been in constant employ since spring, repairing the extensive damage in homes and businesses caused by last winter's extreme weather.

Of course snow and ice are needed to facilitate the fun winter sports like skiing, skating and ice fishing, but to my knowledge, no way has been discovered yet to change or control the jet stream and direction of wind and storms. Since this is not possible, temperature and precipitation can only be estimated thus making it necessary to keep your plans for winter activities flexible.

So far the season has been unusual, but it's not over yet. Keep your salt and shovel handy and pick out some interesting reading material just in case you find yourself housebound. Add a supply of firewood and hot chocolate and don't forget some birdseed for the feeders.

A cozy fire and a warm afghan to curl up with can ease the discomfort of winter when it does arrive, and it will – it always does!

A new year is here; it's time for fresh start

This is that unique time of the year when you have a chance to start fresh once again. It's called 'do-over' time.

If it wasn't accomplished last year, and you still think it's a worthwhile idea, put it on this year's list. Don't make your list the same as last year. Make a new list of possibilities.

I have a few suggestions for you before you list your goals:

1. Don't say, "I'll never," it's such a long time, and too intimidating. "I'll try to" is a better possibility.
2. "I'll always-" is another tough goal. "Less often" or "more often", is more attainable.
3. Trying to improve your own lifestyle is important. Learning a new skill or trying a new avenue of adventure.
4. If you have a skill or talent, promise to teach it to someone else.

5. Teach a child something new. Make the child smile and bring enjoyment to his life.
6. First learn to love yourself and take pride in what you do.
7. Help someone who has no one else to help them. Become a friend and lead him or her to improvement of life.
8. Promise yourself to take more walks in the fresh air and enjoy nature.
9. Set aside a specific time regularly to be good to yourself. It's okay to be a little selfish. You deserve some loving care.

10. If your goal is to improve an area like diet, smoking, reducing stress, controlling anger, aim at a short-term improvement. A year can seem daunting, but a month, a week or even a day at a time is much easier. Then you can increase the improvement for another month or week or even a day.

11. Get to know a neighbor or a shut-in. The joy you give can be returned in an unusual feeling of joy for yourself.

    Most important, take steps to care for your own health, so you can be around to take on more goals next year.

    Remember, if you fall short in your expectations, it's an opportunity to "do it over" again.

Nothing more important in life than your given name

One of the most important things you are given at birth is your brand-new, unblemished name. It is yours only, to do with during your lifetime as you wish. What you say and do affects the purity of your name and develops your reputation.

W hen you are a child, its value may elude you and as a teenager you may not always view life seriously. Bravado, brash attitude and peer pressure often lead to unwise decisions due to immaturity and lack of wisdom. Yet these actions are charged against your reputation account.

Your good name reflects on more than one person. It affects a mother, father, siblings, friends and associates. Reputations are sometimes dependent on the company you keep. Unsavory companions can affect your thoughts, beliefs, language and activities.

Peer pressure is a dominant force. You want to be accepted by your friends, but sometimes the choices you are asked to make are questionable to you. A tough call when you are a teenager!

Nothing brings honor to your family more than to have others commend your behavior or accomplishments. Pride in your family and a desire to achieve can be a driving force.

It is important to feel accepted. It is also important to value your self-worth. If you know you are giving your best effort and it is not harming another individual, you deserve a pat on the back for that effort.

Each of the entrants at the Olympics this year spent long periods of time training, practicing and preparing for their individual event. No one entered the Olympic venues with a desire to lose! Yet there could be only one gold for each event and many factors were affecting the performances. Heat, humidity, state of health, injury, position on the field and emotional strength had to be overcome. Many entrants were disappointed when they were not among the medallists, but had every right to be proud of the fact they were considered competent enough to even be chosen to participate.

Some names will enter the history books, while other names will be proudly honored in a hometown as the chosen one from that town.

The Bible implies that a good name is to be desired more than silver or gold. Much consideration should be given to anything that may cast a shadow on something as important as your name.

Winter is gone; don't let spring pass you by

Are you ready for spring yet? Have you been watching closely for signs? One sign that wasn't fitting was more snow!

I'm thinking more about a first robin, crocuses popping up, buds on the forsythia bushes. Other eyes may see new kittens and puppies, spring lambs, and newly plowed fields anticipating crops to be planted. The winter crop of new babies would be parading in their carriages along with the Christmas wagons and tricycles being peddled as fast as little feet can pump the pedals.

All of these are harbingers of spring though seen from different perspectives. Spring is a time for thought transition from heavy coats and snow shovels to warm breezes and flower gardens. We've made the leap into spring by pushing our clocks ahead to give us longer daylight hours for baseball games, spring clean-up jobs, and planning time for summer vacations, all much happier thoughts than another depressing snowstorm.

Events of your winter may have made it seem longer than it was, but now it's a new day and time to make the spring adjustment. Each day will be tucked full of surprises. We just have to observe and discover them. Listen for the music of spring and see the bright colors of nature. Keep your eyes looking ahead and your mind open to new ideas or you'll miss so much. Winter is gone, but don't let spring pass you by.

Shouldn't be afraid of making changes

Why do you do some things the same all your life? Is it because your mother or father has always done it that way?

While there may be more than one efficient way to achieve a given result, most of us are such creatures of habit we never consider changing our method. Change opens opportunities that could be overlooked if we never veer from our rutted path of ritual.

Your path or route of travel to work each day may be chosen for speed. If you walk, a different route could add blocks of needed exercise if you plan to leave home a few minutes early. You could always take the shorter route in inclement weather.

Driving on a changed route may reveal a less congested drive and be a less stressful way to start your day.

Even something as routine as your pattern of attacking a grocery store could give results. If you map out the store you may find you can skip several aisles and arrive at the checkout much sooner.

Changing your normal routine can both add interest in a job or create a short cut and a saving of time.

Those inclined to add some exercise to their lives could take the stairs instead of waiting for the elevator.

Picking a different place to eat lunch can introduce a different menu and perhaps new personalities to meet.

A change in hairstyle, shortened, curled or colored, can make a significant change in your appearance and the way people perceive you. While you are looking for ways to change, you might consider continuing your education and even career.

It's easy to see how one change can be a starting point to further changes. Perhaps we have thought about changing our lives but never had the courage or incentive to pursue our ideas. Give it some thought and list some of the changes you might consider. Some of these ideas might be worthy of second consideration. You may find you are content to stay where you are and continue your life happily in your usual manner, but maybe at this point in your life you are ready for change, it's never too late.

Protect freedoms we have

In America, each of us is born with the privilege of free will and the right to choose.

We don't have to think alike or like the same things, but that's what makes life interesting. If everyone thought the same life might get boring. If everyone liked the same things life might get monotonous, and we wouldn't have need of 150 television channels. Suppose everyone wore the same type of clothes and the same hairstyle – who would be the trendsetters? If everyone wanted to do the same job, many jobs would be left undone.

We each have a destiny to fulfill. Each of us may prepare for it following a different pathway. One might choose college, another on the job training; one mother may be a stay-at-home mom while another is a career mom; one may choose self-employment and one may choose to work for others.

Success has different forms also. For one person it may be riches; for a second a title or recognition; others may be most rewarded by giving of themselves such as a physician or an educator and some are made happy by giving everything for the good of others.

While some people choose to coast along in life, others are on the fast track, rushing to get to the finish line first.

Not everyone can be the CEO in a company but we can all have the opportunity to strive for it. A few select persons have traveled in space or walked on the moon, but thousands have taken part in preparing the way contributing to the success of the projects.

There can be only one president or mayor or head of a department, but your one vote may be the deciding one to elect that person. That may seem like a minimal effort but it is extremely important.

Did you contribute to the well being of our community by helping the best person in your opinion obtain the office of choice?

If you neglected to vote, you should not have the privilege of criticizing those elected that were not your choice.

We should zealously protect the freedoms we have that are not shared by other countries. Your opinion may differ from others, but it is your privilege to express it.

Where are the Family Values today?

What has happened to the old family values that were so essential to life in past years? Families are described today as single parent, fatherless, split family, divided care, shared care, relative foster care and a variety of other terms. It all means the children are not being cared for in one house by both parents at the same time. Is this just the way it is in the 90's? Does this produce confidant, self-assured, emotionally adjusted children? I think not!

Many adults today are selfishly seeking what they think is best for themselves, not giving concern to what is best for the offspring they have introduced into a hectic world. More children and adults seem to be receiving treatment for emotional problems and depression than at any other time. It seems to be the simplistic answer to say—"It's not my fault, I'm a single parent, or divorced, I'm too stressed to pay attention to the kids all the time, when do I get time just to be me?"

It seems lacking in responsibility to attempt to become a parent when you have not considered the enormity of the task. This is a human life, to be nurtured and loved, to teach, to provide food and shelter for, to keep from harm and provide security, as well as guidance and answers to questions on a daily basis. It requires two loving and devoted parents, working together selflessly for a helpless child who is entirely dependent upon them and did not request admission to this world.

This is God's gift to parents whom He trusts with this burden. In return you will receive love untold and joy you cannot have imagined from such a tiny child. This is a life that you can help mold and influence with your values through your words and actions, to become a useful member of our future society—an awesome task!

Blame is being placed on violence and lack of good role models on television or the friends of your children who may belong to gangs associated with vandalism or drugs.

Are you willing to let others control your children's' lives or will you fight to retain the responsibility for them? Too many of our children are seeing the despair of a loveless home without the security of caring parents. It's never too late to take control to salvage our most precious commodities—our children.

Clean-up Day – One giant yard sale

Pretty soon that annual pilgrimage will be evident in our town. It's called Clean-up Day. For some of us it is 'throw-out day' and we wait patiently every year for the opportunity to get rid of our accumulations. This is the thinking scope for those who like tidy lives and neat garages, or at least less cluttered ones! But for others, it's heralded as a rite of spring. There may be stars all over the calendar marking the day, lest we forget. It's a major shopping day, without the VISA card!

The junk of one family becomes the treasure of another. Most interested are those with creative talents that see past the chipped and broken to the renewed, refinished, reusable item that would be just right for them.

This event is usually one week long so everyone has time to assemble their 'shoppers display. Long before the first clean-up truck comes along though, the pile you had, diminishes greatly. Matter of fact, if it's still on your curbside, you know it must be junk!

If you have a talent for carpentry, recaning, refinishing, repainting, re-upholstering or just a simple need of an extra bicycle, stroller or sofa, this could be an enjoyable search. Not only in your own neighborhood, but watch the newspapers for clean-up days in neighboring towns.

When you discover that one great treasure in your search, it usually makes up for any embarrassment of junk picking. Incidentally, this search usually begins at dusk and continues through the cover of night. It amazes some people to find most of their contributions gone by daylight.

The price of new items, and often extra things you really don't need may be cost prohibitive. This fact has developed a new generation for shoppers. They are on the move most Fridays and Saturdays, frequenting the multiple garage sales. Clean-up day is an extended giant garage sale.

So collect YOUR junk first and deposit it on your curb. Make a rule in your house that for every 'new' piece coming into your house, there must be one old piece leaving—just to keep the garage neat! If the new treasure doesn't work out, or if it still hasn't been 'renewed' within a year, you can always place it on your curb next year on clean-up day.

Change is Tough

It's tough to make changes, some in our thinking and some in how we do things.

Sure it's easier to do it 'your' way, because you've done it so often you know your way best. That doesn't mean there isn't a better way. If someone else had to learn your way, it might be difficult for them. When different results are needed, brains race to find a different or better way to achieve them. If fewer people are available to do a job, a more effective method may be needed to get the job completed and it may prove to be more efficient.

New blood often brings new ideas to a company or organization. Old methods can become so routine the new ways are not even considered or thought necessary.

Sometimes a new method may be introduced so insidiously it is hardly noticed until the result is seen.

When businesses merge, often many changes are made. Some necessary, some simply desired. Personnel managers can introduce changes in various ways:

1. My way or the highway.
2. It is necessary to make some changes. This is how we are going to do it. An instructor will help you learn the new method.
3. Keep things the same temporarily, then make gradual changes.

As long as an improvement or a better result can be proven, change may be readily accepted.

As generations of people change, their needs and desires change. The current generation is computer driven. It is imperative to be knowledgeable if you are to have an active part in businesses today. Schools are beginning classes with the very youngest students. If you are a grandparent, don't be surprised if your grandchild knows more about computers than you. Procedures that took many steps when you learned them are done almost instantly by computers today. It's important to know how procedures are done and to carefully instruct a computer how to perform the same function. Many man-hours can be saved if the computer is instructed correctly, but the person feeding the information to the computer must be very accurate or incorrect data will be the end result. If older or more experienced employees make the effort to become computer literate, they may be the best choice to feed data into computer programs.

Since computers function round the clock, often companies can produce more by having staff instruct computers during later hours than offices usually work and have reports or statistics prepared before morning staff arrives in the morning ready for their analysis.

Young adults may have an advantage with companies today since most of them have studied computer sciences in school and are more likely to be knowledgeable about the latest advances.

If older employees, no matter how loyal, have not kept abreast with computerization, they may find they are not as valuable to a company as they thought. Their areas of experience may have to be transferred to other departments and the job description may not be the one they prefer. It's a tough realization. Technology has changed the business world drastically, but knowledge of your company, its' products and customers will always be valued. Prepare for your future by keeping informed and willing to accept change if it is shown to be useful or necessary so you'll be able to charge into the twenty-first century with enthusiasm.

Do you really mean it when you declare that resolution?

How long was your list of New Year's resolutions? Was it short and sweet, listing only the essentials? Or was it wistfully long and unattainable?

Some people would rather change jobs or even a spouse than change themselves. It isn't easy changing an ingrained habit or a long-standing manner of doing things. Most of us would prefer that others accommodate our needs than us have to accommodate theirs.

When you listed your resolutions, was it for a major life change or did you attack your list with a realistic viewpoint?

Was the first: Lose 25 pounds? That sounds so difficult to accomplish it will probably be ditched before one week has passed. It might be easier to stick with it if you resolved to eat healthier, exercise and set a goal for two pounds a month. Too easy you say? Try it, persevere and surprise yourself with results.

A second one: Always be on time! Maybe an effort to get up a half-hour earlier or leave for work earlier would be easier to attain.

Save more money! That's always a good one. But just limiting your 'charges' to one card at a time and vow not to charge more until that one is paid off would be a good start.

While you're looking for sweeping life changes, try to include a resolution to reward yourself when you accomplish a goal. If it's the 'lose weight' one, there could be a tasty treat, 'cause you earned it!

Another tough one might deal with a relationship with a neighbor or co-worker. Everything might not be completely rosy everyday, but it might be a little easier to try looking for some 'little' thing that's likeable about that person. I know it means effort – but it will mean keeping another resolution.

If temptation makes you slide the first month, cross that month off and start anew the next month, but don't give up.

Once you get to be successful at this game of improvement, don't be surprised if people start reacting differently to you, and that could bring out the best in them too.

Recycling isn't so New after all is Said and Done

Recycling is not really such a new thing to do in our society. Many of us have recycled for years without thinking about it.

Many things in my house have 'gone around' and are 'coming around' again. Sometimes it is a piece of furniture that gets repainted, refinished or re-upholstered and finds a new room or even our children's houses to live in.

Curtains and drapes are always recycled when you move to a new house – some to new windows and some to a local rummage sale.

Children's clothing found its way to a younger child or relative as well as toys that were outgrown. If it was not yours before, it was new to you. Some of the toys have been recycled for other uses. Sleds pull heavy boxes or baskets around the yard and toy wagons haul a myriad of things that used to be hand-carried. Even dollhouse furniture can become a collection of miniatures.

Baskets never get thrown out at my house. I've found them to be useful for so many things from holding plants and flowers to storing clothes or toys.

Dolls were re-vamped in our household rather than thrown away by acquiring a new wardrobe or sometimes a new wig.

The good cooks in my neighborhood were usually talked out of some of their greatest recipes as the new brides were learning to cook.

Even a garden gets recycled as a compost heap is established to live again in other areas of the yard next year.

Our family is addicted to reading and everyone knows how quickly books can accumulate. Some were re-read by family members, but many were traded to friends and neighbors before the advent of garage sales.

Probably the biggest recycling effort of several decades ago was cloth diapers. Today's mothers cannot imagine even physically handling soiled diapers, much less laundering them and refolding to be used again and again. Several children were usually recipients of the same batch of diapers although each sibling wore them slightly thinner than the last or doubled. Today a major shopping item is disposable diapers. How many mothers of the 50's or 60's dreamed of throwing away a diaper after one use? The biggest luxury of that era was a mobile diaper service that would replace your soiled diapers with fresh clean cloth diapers once or twice weekly. Now the disposable diapers are seen as a threat to recycling because they do not readily deteriorate in landfills.

Aluminum soda cans are saved now, but formerly beverages were bottled in glass and the bottles were collected and re-used again.

Many ideas that appear to be new innovations are not really so new after all, but if they can be improved upon, it may continue to keep our planet from being cluttered.

Exchanging of Ideas, Experiences Important

What are you really like? Do other people like to be around you? Do you complain a lot? Do you monopolize the conversation or do you listen? We can't be learning much if we are talking all the time. Knowledge results from the exchange of ideas and experiences.

Many of us know seniors that are fun to be around, wearing a smile, with something upbeat and interesting to talk about or maybe even a joke to share. Cheerful as that person may seem to be, certainly some rain or hardship has visited his or her life. But somehow they choose to look at the upper, more sunny side of life and move on in a positive manner.

We all have a choice. We can choose to grumble, grouse and complain, or we can deal with our problems constructively. Either choice we make, surely the sun will rise in the morning and the world will continue to spin.

Many of our senior citizens have a wealth of information and experiences to pass on to the present generation. Often we ignore them because they tend to repeat the same stories or take forever to finish telling them, but unless we do listen, much family history and knowledge will leave this world untold.

Just by casual listening I have learned many tales of history in my own family that had never before been divulged. Some have dealt with talent and accomplishments I would otherwise not have known.

I would not presume to visualize anyone sitting daily by the hour trying to glean some little gem of information from a parent or grandparent. No one can be expected to be that patient and saintly. But regular short visits perhaps with a few pertinent questions to start the conversation may yield the treasures of that person's life. You may discover a famous accomplishment to be able to pass on to your children someday. These regular short visits can bring untold joy to the elderly senior whose world may have shrunk to severe limits in later years. It is sad indeed to view the many residents of nursing homes, cut off from normal socialization, that long for a visitor to talk with or smile with even for 15 minutes in a day. The memory of that visit lasts much longer with them than the brief 15 minutes you spent. If you bring a fistful of flowers from your garden, the memory lasts even longer as they relive it through the fragrance of the bouquet.

We will all age. Science has not discovered a way to stop it. Maybe we can cover up a sign or two, but eventually it arrives. If you are one of the cheery-agers, you may find your daytime hours filled with more friends than if you are a grumpy-ager.

Make your choice, the benefits are many. Don't be the one who hears, "Oh no, look who's coming!"

Use that Extra Hour Wisely

Most everyone complains they never have enough time to do what they would like or even must do. Now, each of us will be given the gift of one extra hour everyday, come this weekend with Daylight Savings Time. Just what we said we needed. What are you planning to do with yours?

You could roll over in the morning and savor one extra hour of sleep.

You could start that exercise or jogging program you've been thinking about.

You could rise early and read to increase your knowledge or just to complete some of those novels you've been meaning to read.

You could spend the time working on a craft or hobby or some project on your ditty list.

You could start your necessary chores earlier to free up one hour or parts of your extra hour to volunteer your help and services to a neighbor or organization.

You could catch up on delayed correspondence.

You could use your hour to enjoy your favorite music or view a beautiful sunrise.

Whatever your choice, if continuous and consistent, it can become a habit of routine you incorporated into your day and can bring you the joy of accomplishment.

This is your moment of opportunity. Even if you continue for one or several months, the challenge of a goal or satisfaction of achievement can be valuable to you.

Today is the day to start spending your precious extra hour. Make your choice carefully, spend it wisely and enjoy it.

Ordinary People can be Significant People

It doesn't take fantastic effort. It doesn't even take an unusual talent. It is something we are all capable of achieving.

Each of us can make a difference some place in someone's life. We each have that talent, though it may not be readily recognized.

Can you remember that one person in your neighborhood that attracted all the children to her house? Exciting things were always happening there. Sometimes it was a fun game or a unique project, maybe a new craft everyone learned, or how to paint or draw. That person made you feel special – made you feel like you could do almost anything if you tried hard enough.

Do you remember a person that always had time to listen to you as you told about your fears, your dreams, or your feelings? Do you remember a neighbor who was never too busy to do an errand, care for a child or pet, lend a helping hand when you needed it most, but seemed otherwise so ordinary?

Do you recall the special man or woman that always was able to volunteer when needed and never seemed to be too busy, but they thought they never did anything important?

Each of these people is ordinary in so many ways, yet special, if only to you. You are special to someone, although you may not be aware of it. Locate your particular talent. It may surprise you to know just what it is. You could be responsible for having a definite effect in someone's life. Whatever that ability is, please keep on doing it during this year and help make a significant difference in your corner of the world.

A pat on the Back to the Generous Snow Souls are in order

How much shoveling did you have to do? More than you wanted to do, I'm sure.

Did you think others were shoveling their share? Did you find yourself fighting for space to put 'your' snow when someone else was using that same space?

It has been a horrendous problem for everyone. An even bigger problem for those who are responsible for making it disappear completely before the next storm brings a fresh supply. I don't know where they are taking it, but it's almost like magic to wake in the morning and find large quantities have been removed. It sure does help to be able to see through an intersection before you are halfway across it.

Snow like this brings out the best and worst of personalities. I have heard many complaining about everything, from unshoveled snow to empty shelves in grocery stores. I've also seen many people who have gone far out of their way to come to the aid of neighbors and elderly, sometimes to shovel, sometimes to deliver or transport them in emergencies. We can almost bet our taxes will rise to subsidize the horrific costs of caring for the roads during these current storms. One bright spot I observed during the extraordinarily long days of the town's plowing and our shoveling occurred when my husband had just completed clearing our driveway of the 'street' snow once again. I saw the town plow doing its job on our street and just as he approached our driveway, he raised the plow blade until he passed, then lowered it again. I shouted a grateful "thank you" but it probably was not heard.

Fortunately we don't deal with storms like these very often. It sure is nice to know there are many good

Samaritans in our area and all of them deserve a pat on the back and a big thank you for their generosity.

This time of year, 'S' word often takes Center Stage

These thoughts will deal with the "S" word. It is the season of the year when we all have to deal with a little more of it than usual. The secret is how we choose to deal with it. Can you make a guess? Yes – STRESS!

Heading the list will be dealing with relatives for the holidays. Do you visit them? Do you invite them to visit you? Will it have to be separate visits to accommodate the ones that aren't speaking? Whose turn is it? Is that even important?

Holiday celebrations have changed over the years. Young families were expected to travel long distances to spend Christmas Day at grandma's house. Parents and children were required to pack and travel for hours to meet family obligations. Today's family may have mom and dad both working until the day before the holiday and necessitate great planning plus running shoes to achieve the same task. Holiday preparations at home are often not noticed until the day after Christmas when you are too tired to appreciate the effort.

Traveling itself creates stress since winter weather can be so unpredictable. How about staying at home and inviting neighbors who may not be able to see their families to share the day with you. It could start a community trend.

Stress can take on many faces: crankiness, a short temper, changes in disposition or forgetfulness because there is too much to do.

Which brings us to Christmas shopping. Do we really have to stretch our credit limits every year to buy expensive gifts? Why not give a 'self' gift, offering to do a chore or errand or even just a Christmas visit with some homemade cookies? It is an alternative to searching for hours for the perfect gift for someone who may or may not appreciate the effort.

Some families may be experiencing economic crises this year. It could be the perfect time to have a homemade or self-gift Christmas.

Holiday parties can even be more fun with less work if the menu is shared with some of the guests. Your shut–in neighbor might consider it a treat to address your greeting cards and be kept busy for a day.

Most important of all is to remember the reason for the season. IT IS ABOUT LOVE. Giving your love because it has been given to you.

Do something special for your self, because you deserve it. Then do something special for a stranger. It may be the only "gift" they receive.

Finding your Comfort Zone takes a Little Work

Have you ever tried to locate your comfort zone? It can vary sharply. Some people need more 'space' than others.

You probably know someone that is an academic leader or excels in business and you may also know someone who would never crave the limelight, but prefer a behind the scenes position. We need both for balance. If there are no leaders, how will we know whom to follow? If there are no followers, then a leader isn't effective.

Occasionally someone lives in a false comfort zone. He or she may reside in a city atmosphere trying to cope with a chaotic lifestyle, molding a life to please a parent in an inappropriate career. Hopefully, they may recognize the misfit of their pursuit in time to change courses and follow a more satisfying path.

The same people that enjoy science and research may not have any interest in creative arts, while creative arts devotees may not be able to balance a checkbook. Most people strive to strike a happy balance between the extremes and find a middle road for their comfort zone. It is important to find that comfortable area.

Today it is possible to explore many career areas via computer, locating the pluses and minuses of a variety of careers before entering the field. The opportunity for education in the varied careers is also available via computer, so opportunities are more accessible than pre-computer days.

Career counselors can often guide you to an area of expertise you never thought to explore. We don't always recognize our own talents or potential. Everyone cannot be at ease in the same circumstances. Wherever we are at present is the place to make our happiness count. Explore and observe the many comfort areas that already surround us. It is important to recognize them in order to enjoy life to the fullest.

Always Great to Win, whether it's Bridge or Golf

It's always great to be a winner. Whether it's a bridge game, a golf game or the Boston Marathon foot race, everyone asks, who won. Of course this means someone has to be second, but no one seems to ask who came in second.

There is a certain thrill about competing that races your heart and causes the adrenaline to flow faster. Wouldn't it be nice to have a trophy or prize just for trying? It sure would make more people happy. Everyone has to train or practice for a competition. The second and third placers have trained just as hard, and all participants try to win with all their available energy and effort.

In life, if we choose not to try because we might not win, nothing will ever be accomplished. Great discoveries and research projects would fail because we lack confidence in ourselves. Many discoveries are made in medicine quite by accident, while looking for other answers.

If we have a desire to compete in any area- sports, research, school, business or socially, we must first set our goal to compete, prepare for the race, practice for the event and set our minds with a positive attitude. If you fail to be first, you have not failed in the attempt, you have gained knowledge, discipline, physical fitness and the joy of competing. You also just might be the winner this time!

The Intrusion

At first it begins as an unhappiness within your skull, an imbalance of the equanimity of life, gradually growing into a definite discontent.

Slowly, but deliberately, it proceeds to stamp its' feet and tramp from one side of the space to another. The space becomes crowded, but still the thump of stamping feet continues. Soon it becomes so top-heavy from the weight of multiplying feet; it takes two hands to support it.

Two smooth rounded pills are introduced into an opening below the misery.

After a virtual eternity, the stamping becomes plodding, then scuffling, and finally, mercifully, ends.

A peaceful tranquility consumes the space. Contentment returns to the beleaguered skull. The headache is gone!

It's called Sport!

It may be as cold as it 'is', but not necessarily as cold as it's going to 'get'.

Winter's first day has come, so cold is expected now, it almost has permission now – after all – it's winter!

The first day is the shortest day of the year. Actually it's still twenty-four hours long. It doesn't even seem shorter when it's cold. The sun is at the lowest angle on the horizon and as far away from us that it can get. More of the twenty-four hours are in darkness on the first day of winter. But cheer up, if you lived at the North Pole you'd see a lot more darkness and for a longer time than you did in New Jersey.

Darkness I can deal with; coldness is another matter. There are just so many layers of clothing one can fit on one body. I know, they say 'layer' – that's the secret. I can tell you from personal experience, there are some days there are not enough layers in this state that would keep me warm.

It happened on the first day of ice-fishing season several years ago. One of those lovely icy cold days, with a most bitter wind blowing off the lake. I remember it like it was yesterday. Some members of my family talked me into participating in the 'sport' of ice fishing. Believe me when I say it is perverse to call this 'SPORT'.

We thought we were prepared for everything. Our equipment was in working order—the auger, tip-ups, bait, even hot chocolate, sandwiches and a special stove to keep us warm while we were on the ice. I should have been suspicious then. We moved around a lot. Got all the holes drilled and set-up. We baited the lines and skimmed the ice from the holes. Drank some hot-hot chocolate, jumped up and down, clapped our hands and stamped our feet, checked the holes regularly, and drank more not-so-hot chocolate. Finally after several hours of this 'fun' with no results, we decided to go home and do something more sane!

After what seemed like the longest hot shower of my life, I still wasn't warm. As I recall, I really don't think I warmed up until June that year!

Haven't been ice-fishing since that day. If you drive past any local lake this winter, don't look for me. I won't be there. I've decided fishing should be done in the summer!

The Naked 'Edge

Having discussed trimming our overgrown hedge for several years, my husband and I made a decision to "Do it now!"

The monstrosity covered half the length of the house and had grown well above the windowsills. We weren't sure where to start, how to start or how much to cut, but armed with determination and enthusiasm, we attacked aggressively.

Starting with 'a little off the top,' we advanced to 'shaping the external line,' and eventually got around to hacking mercilessly, as we realized how much pruning was necessary due to many years of neglect.

After two hours of steady labor, we stepped back to survey our progress and could only stand in shocked silence. The nearest comparison that came to mind was Bonsai tree! It had a definite naked appearance.

Our son drove into the driveway and with great facial control, politely observed, "I see you've trimmed the hedge."

The size of the pile of discarded branches was almost larger than the remaining scalped hedge.

Since that day, we've learned not to prune during the season we had chosen, not to prune during dry weather spells and several other knowledgeable facts. What we did achieve was some feeling of accomplishment—we have become the neighborhood attraction, however infamous, and we have made the neighbors' hedges look 'better than that one!' We also don't have an ugly, overgrown monster since we've converted it to a Japanese counterpart, the Bonsai Bush!

Wait Till Next Year

That's what we've done!

Last year we waited and waited and almost gave up hope before that first snow. This year I already hear cries of enough already! And winter has not even arrived!

We can blame it on the jet stream, or upper atmospheric disturbances, but it still boils down to shoveling.

Last Saturday I knew if my share of snow was not moved that day, by Sunday it would become an immovable object and unfortunately it was a correct assumption. This snow promises more of the same by topping off the beautiful white fluffy stuff with a light layer of rain to hold it in place, perhaps for weeks if the thermometer doesn't become unstuck. Doesn't your heart bleed for those poor unfortunates in Florida who can't get into the spirit of Christmas because of all that boring green grass to look at and that uncomfortable heat they're dealing with—wouldn't it be nice to try it for awhile? Remember, we didn't much like all the heat we had this past summer.

Well, this too shall pass—maybe not quickly enough for some, but look at the bright side--some people love the stuff. Skiing, sleigh riding, ice-skating, snow-mobiling, (if you didn't sell it after last year), and don't forget ice-fishing and ice-boating as some of the fun healthy activities many folks enjoy. Others take on an indoor project this time of year and hunker down with a good book or craft to do while assuming the couch-potato position. Of course, if you're really ambitious, there are all those closets and drawers you've been meaning to clean out, but then they'll still be there after the hot chocolate and the good book are finished.

Holiday in the Pits

Lounging around for weeks before and after the holidays with no real agenda could sound like Utopia. No shopping, cooking, hustling around, decorating or visiting sounds restful. Could be – unless it's inflicted on you suddenly by the universal holiday germ!

"The Germ" descended on my once healthy body early in December and made itself so much at home that it moved in permanently for the entire holiday season. I guess it was my fault for being so hospitable and providing a place for it to live. It really settled in with all its luggage—weekender, large and small carry-ons and a trunk! My non-domestic husband became a necessary 'Susie-homemaker' adding much stress to his life and holiday spirit.

The first two days in bed were enough time for 'fetching and doing' to wear thin, but by then 'IT' was just settling down into the soft pillows and getting ready to establish roots for expansion. The tentacles spread to a larger space in my body making more aching feelings and harsh sounds fill my surrounding space. Days turned into weeks, the supply of medicines and potions increased across my shelf and still each day brought some new surprise to attack the weakening mass I had become. Antibiotics came and went. Sprays and syrups, capsules, pills and liquids all took their turn on that medicine shelf. Relentlessly, 'IT' kept me busy coughing, aching, slurping soup, wheezing, sweating, freezing and occasionally sleeping.

My social life, being drastically curtailed, was limited to doctors' office waiting rooms, hospital x-ray lounges and drug store visits. Not the best choices if you're seeking some holiday cheer, but encouraging in the sense that these places were full, so I knew I wasn't singled out.

Friends and relatives called on the phone and some even thought my germs were transmitted via phone lines when they became sick just days later. No one was brave enough to come to the door, not even salesmen! Some small blessing there somewhere!

My touch with the outside world was enhanced by a large bay window, overlooking a wooded area. Daily visitors were squirrels, birds, wild turkeys and neighborhood cats. Each assured me the world was continuing to spin.

Weather changed from exceptionally mild, to wild winter snowstorm with wind and ice and finally settled on just plain steady cold.

My moods swung from passive, to anxious, to irritated, resigned, depressed and finally to promising encouragement by the time all the medicine bottles were empty.

One morning I woke up and actually felt I was making progress. No sweating during the night, no aching, no coughing, like I said, progress! New year, new lease on life, new hope for a better year.

I checked for 'IT's' luggage and didn't find it – 'IT's gone—GOOD!

Goose Crossing

The cars ahead of me flashed a staccato of red brake lights and then a constant blare of red lights as they stopped completely. As I stretched my neck into a better viewing position, I saw a large congregation of Canadian geese in various stages of crossing the farm road to a vacant field.

"Goose-in-charge" was honking loudly as he waddled back and forth just daring the cars to come closer, as he directed his gaggle across the road. Eventually they all made their journey safely to the flat field and "goose-in-charge" honked his final retorts and waddled after them as traffic resumed on the road.

Filling up your Holiday

Alone for the holidays is more than lonesome. It makes a person feel that nobody wants to be their friend. It is empty, sad and depressing.

There are many people who are alone, or at least have nothing to do on the holidays either because of the distance from friends and relatives or the absence of friends and relatives.

There are several things to do to correct this situation:

A. Sit at home and mope, feeling sorry for yourself and becoming further depressed.

B. Go to where the people are, whether your friends or not, soon you may make friends with the other 'friendless' or lonely people.

During the holiday seasons there are usually centers that concentrate on providing a meal and warmth of friendship. It might be a town recreation hall or a local church. Not all people you meet are friendless, many are compassionate volunteers who just like to do something for others. Often a whole family will volunteer to serve meals or provide recreation, songs, games and chatter.

Radio shows sometimes advertise the holiday centers or newspapers list activities of a church or community for gathering to celebrate a holiday. Many churches offer candlelight services followed by caroling. People do not need to know each other to join a group in a church or community center.

If you really want to be around people during the holidays there are many opportunities. You can easily become a volunteer—groups never refuse a helping hand.

Last year several groups gathered warm coats and sweaters along with blankets and went to areas of known homelessness to distribute these items. Homeless people don't like to ask for help but it is always welcome when it's offered.

Organizations, whether church oriented or Salvation Army sponsored are always looking for people to help them be helpful. This could be your chance to make someone else's holiday be cheerful. You will probably be surprised at how good it makes you feel.

Sharing an Adventure

Wouldn't it be fun to have an adventure? Where would it take you? Who would go with you? I wouldn't like to go alone I don't think. Much more fun having someone to share a sight, a sunset, or an experience. I wouldn't go to a place of little interest to me. Some would love Alaska—I think I'd rather enjoy the Grand Canyon and the Indian villages, or California wine country. Of course there's Paris and China for major trips, but I could see what is closer at hand much sooner.

An adventure needs planning. First you need a longing to go to a special place, then time to prepare for the trip. Maybe research about the area so you can plan what sights to see. A trip is more satisfying if you are familiar with the destination. You don't want to come home and find out you missed a major attraction.

If your adventure is to an island or country that speaks a different language it gives an opportunity and challenge to learn conversational phrases. You might even pursue a night class before you go to enhance your fluency.

Excitement builds each day while you are gathering your knowledge and preparing for your trip.

What do you think you know about your adventure choice? Where can you find out more about it? How long should you stay? Fly or go by cruise: What clothes do you take? Good excuse to buy new ones - if you need an excuse!

Make sure you take a camera. You can relive your trip again with your friends.

Now it's time to buy the ticket! That marks the real beginning of the trip.

In your lifetime you may often plan to do things but frequently those plans are changed. Circumstances may altar to prevent their completion. It may be health, finances, family obligations or unforeseen misfortune. If you are not able to take your adventure at least buy the ticket in your mind.

Once circumstances allow and you are prepared – take the trip! Savor every step of the way; enjoy every minute, make it worth every minute of your preparation. You bought the ticket – Go For It!

How is your Attitude?

It's been said, that many people who choose not to 'go with the flow' of life, have an 'attitude'. We all have an attitude—it just depends on how we choose to react to daily occurrences. We can be rigid or easy going. We can be perfectionists or casual. We can be happy and see the joyful parts of life or we can choose to be pessimistic, crabby and complain about everything.

For an example, the weather. Sure it's quite hot-but it's supposed to be, it's summer! If it were winter, it would be cold because that's how winter weather is! What makes our weather more hot or more cold is constantly talking about it. We can change our thoughts and concentrate on cool breezes and shady places along with happy occasions throughout the summer and by pre-occupying your thoughts, you won't have time to notice how hot it really is.

Every small town has at least one person who will come into town on the hottest or coldest day and comment to anyone who will listen how hot or cold they are because they walked to town from their home. They could have stayed home with the air-conditioner or fan in summer, or stayed in a warm house in the winter and not walk about town until it was a bit warmer unless it was an emergency.

Some of us must move about in the heat due to our work or responsibilities. While we're out it would make someone who is without a car or elderly very happy if we did some of their errands. It would brighten the day for the person at home and would certainly make us feel better knowing we've helped someone else.

Our world is filled with many people who have more than they need and can afford to buy anything to make them happier. They don't see why they should go out of their way to help others. Perhaps it's a superiority complex or just plain selfishness.

If you own a business and don't have your store open for convenient hours, people will assume you really don't need their business and go elsewhere. This attitude says, I'm more important than you are and you'll have to do things my way or I won't service you. Conversely, if you have a happy disposition and hours that accommodate most people, they will flock to your door and your business will thrive.

When you walk down the street, do you have a frown or a smile on your face? A smile will surely attract a smile from someone else, but a frown will turn people away from you showing disapproval of the message that you don't want to be friendly.

A store that does not have adequate or willing people to wait on you gives that message of not needing your business. Another store that makes a habit of greeting you when you enter and asking if they can help you find what you are looking for usually gets your business next time also.

A smile can even overcome a feeling of shyness. It encourages people to pass a greeting or start a conversation. We all respond to smiling faces more favorably than grouchy or sullen attitudes.

There are some solitary professions in which a person may work alone and not come in contact with the public. If they don't care to smile, they don't have to, but even they would feel better if they did.

The professions that deal with many people must attract people who are encouraging and upbeat rather than pessimistic and downbeat. Can you imagine going to a doctor's office and hearing gloom and doom every visit? If you're smart, you'll find another doctor or the gloom and doom doctor will make you sicker. It is apparent in healing to have a positive attitude or a patient will have no incentive to feel better.

It has been shown that even patients with devastating diseases tend to rally and some even extend their lives or become cured simply through a positive mental attitude. Your mind and attitude really do make a big difference in how you feel.

One sure way to live longer is to be an optimist. Always seeing a brighter tomorrow or a happy ending will greatly influence the hormonal effects in your body. It even stimulates and releases pain-killing qualities in your brain to give you a feeling of well–being.

Controlling your attitude toward your daily living will also have an effect on your children and other members of your family. It's difficult to remain morose in the company of some bright spirited person who is intent on not letting you be. Give yourself an opportunity to observe life from another viewpoint.

Take a walk in the sunshine, smile at others, hear the sounds of nature and surround yourself with upbeat people. You'll find you can't help but feel better.

What Makes Great Kids?

Are great kids just born that way or are they the product of a privileged atmosphere?

Pressure is severe when a parent is super successful and presses a child to follow either the same vocation or chooses a vocation for the child.

Some times when a child's life turns off course and he becomes a problem at school or a problem with society, his home-life or upbringing is blamed. Other children could be the product of alcoholic parents or a broken home left to provide for themselves with a minimum of resources and persevere under the most adverse conditions yet become a true asset to their community.

Some kids have an extraordinary amount of pluck and stubbornly pursue life regardless of the tough times they encounter. They don't blame circumstances; they just start out again in a different direction and try to improve their chances. Many of these same young people set examples of leadership and caring for their peers and community. It just comes from within and a desire to succeed at something.

It is surprising to see a disadvantaged youngster rise above his adversity and become a useful and respected citizen. Often many people in the community have a hand in encouraging and guiding the young person needing help. It might be a neighbor, teacher or Scout leader, but someone who believes there is potential to be tapped and tries to reach for it, drawing it out of a child who never had self-esteem.

If you get the opportunity to offer some encouragement to a young friend who might need a little guidance, seize the moment. You'll be glad you did. The recipient might not realize your effort until later in life, but will be pleased that someone saw the potential and helped him achieve a feeling of worth.

Spring Runway

The current styles are being shown on the international runways with the latest fashions for the new couture season. The beautiful people are lined up in the best seats getting a glimpse of the finest, created by the most notable designers. It may feature long flowing skirts or tight-fitting minis. There may be colorful prints, bright colors or monochromatic black and white.

The creative minds have worked endlessly throughout the previous months, cutting and draping a variety of the finest fabrics to create the latest sensation in the fashion world. Each one hoping their design will be the favorite choice of the season, however extreme it may be.

Do you personally know anyone person who will be buying and wearing an original? Probably very few of us do, but we'll try to copy the styles in our choices as they relate to our lifestyle and our budgets.

We really don't have to subscribe to the sheep mentality style, of all following in one direction and wearing a style that does not flatter us simply because a designer said we should.

I don't know about most of you but I need more than a flick of a hairbrush and dab of lipstick to look fabulous. So my suggestion is to go with the classic styles and what you know looks good on your figure and fits in with your lifestyle.

If you feel comfortable in the style you choose, you'll look great and you won't have spent your entire fortune on an outfit that you may wear once and even then not feel entirely comfortable in such high style because you're uncomfortable with the image.

Who's in Charge?

In today's 'Order of the Household', it seems their role of the disciplinarian has shifted greatly. Parents seem to relinquish their position of leader and role model too quickly to public opinion or peer pressure, perhaps because it takes too much effort to prevail over their principles.

The children of these households, left to flounder in the sea of choices have not matured sufficiently to make wise decisions. They often follow in the path of stronger peer leaders. The leaders of our children are not always endowed with wisdom, but rather nerve, aggressive behavior, desperate need and lack of guidance from parents.

Parents of this decade, in general, spend much less time with their small children due to working outside the home, a desire to pursue a career, schooling and demands of society.

Children are being forced into positions of independence at such early ages that childhood, as we once knew it, no longer seems to exist. Children learn to take charge of their lives out of necessity and then resent elders limiting their actions.

If you were a child in the 40's or 50's, did the thought enter your mind to take your parents to court to sue them or more defiantly to divorce them? First of all, your seat would be warmed, your privileges revoked, your chores increased and your life, as you formerly knew it would be changed drastically!

Today, if any of these measures were taken, the doorbell would ring and you would suddenly meet a representative from DYFS! Instead of your child having to explain HIS actions, YOU would be asked to defend YOURS, probably before a judge.

Parents have begun to believe they need every state-of-the art convenience to make life bearable, when finances dictate this is an impossibility. Nevertheless, credit cards somehow make it happen with the delusion that you don't have to pay for it NOW! You DO have to pay for it eventually however and working outside the home may be a temporary necessity. It also means someone else is needed to care for your children or if they are old enough, they may be caring for themselves in your absence. This creates a need for them to make choices and decisions in your absence, all of which may not be wise or safe.

Americans have access to far more technology than any previous generation. While they may wish to avail themselves to it all, finances prohibit this from happening except in affluent societies. It may seem that extra salary will solve this dilemma, but that employment presents extra expense in itself. Carfare or an extra vehicle is needed. A newer wardrobe for the workfield you enter or additional education may be necessary. Less hours at home may require childcare, changes in menu to 'take-out' or prepared foods for economy of time, less family time together and of course, less relaxing time.

New schedules must be made listing priority items at the top of the list. Two family leaders working away from home change many ordinary events. Family members must integrate activities and chores. This does not always happen willingly. Necessities are key, but chores don't always have to be completed to the same standard if time is shortened. Chief responsibility is safe care of small children. It is essential to check references thoroughly for anyone who cares for your children. The ideal would be a family member. Second best, a responsible mature adult that can provide your children a nurturing atmosphere in your absence. Whomever you choose, your children should know they must respect that person's authority until you return home.

Some businesses have instituted a flextime schedule for employees with children so they are not away from their children as much.

Much thought is needed before making these difficult decisions. Let's hope clear heads are weighing all the options and priorities. Children are our most important possessions.

How to Survive the Season

Visual images are always easier to understand. It's easy to imagine an injury from an event like a train wreck or a car crash and the feeling of the pain involved from such injuries. What I can't understand is how miserable you can feel and how totally debilitated a person can be, when something so tiny you cannot see it, somehow invades your body without doing anything more innocuous than breathing! It flattens you immediately, disrupting your life, as you formerly knew it without warning.

You innocently go to bed one night and when you wake in the morning you wonder who has taken over your body! Where is it? You feel effects in so many places it's impossible to be sure of its location. Your eyelids won't open wide. Your head hurts. You cough. Sometimes you have strange and weird sounds when you breathe. Your neck, arms, body, back, legs and everything else just hurts to think about moving them. One germ—virus, bacteria, bug—who knows? Where did it come from?

It invades, searches deep, latches onto the wall with tentacles, irritates, multiplies, destroys and absorbs all your strength. How can something so tiny do so much?

Physicians certainly want you to improve, but the fine line between caution and pressure of drug salesmen to promote new products is tedious.

I'm not a large person and do well on smaller doses of medicine. Maybe the newest and strongest isn't right for me. What will it do to my stomach or equilibrium? Sometimes the cure makes you feel worse. It's important for me to speak up to my doctor so we both are on the same line for health expectations.

Reactions can range from an upset stomach, to hives or headaches. Also reactions to other medicines you may be taking.

Using the more aggressive drugs too soon may decrease its' effectiveness at a later time for a more lethal germ.

My latest germ turned out to be bacteria. Knowing my past history, my doctor introduced a fairly new, but also gentle variety for quick short term. For days it flattened my person and nearly nailed me to my bed, but one night I awoke to the feeling that my troops were ready to drag the flag up the hill and maybe claim victory! By morning, I decided it might be more like a slow crawl, but I would at least be moving! Several more days, strength began to creep in and previous thoughts of near-death were replaced with hopefulness.

Common sense along with diligence to stick to the medical program are absolute necessities.

Viruses do not respond to antibiotics as many people may think. I'm sick, give me an antibiotic! A definite 'no-no' is using someone else's medicine!

It's a rough season for respiratory illnesses during the winter and early spring so be prepared and avoid areas of known infection. Eat well. Get rest and take vaccines if they are recommended by your doctor. If you do get 'bitten', maybe it will turn out to be more of a nibble rather than a major bite out of your health.

View of Nature

You don't actually have to leave your home to experience life in your neighborhood. All you need is a vantagepoint and a view. I have such a view, after years of living in houses with limited view windows. I now can boast an array of thriving plants and flowers that would cause a case of jealous envy even from a disinterested house gardener.

I have lived in my current home almost a year now and deliberately have not disturbed the earth until it could be evenly observed in all seasons. Two enormous bay windows with a southeasterly exposure bring the brilliance of morning to my breakfast table surrounded by a mini-forest of trees that I have observed fully dressed in summer splendor, undressed in winter nakedness and the in-between changing of clothes in fall and spring. It has been a challenge identifying the individual sprouts and buds as they pop into view at weekly and sometimes daily intervals.

My mini-forest has presented its varied residents who visit, some for curiosity, some for food. Red and gray squirrels, groundhogs, rabbits and a devoted pair of gray hawks, as well as a wide variety of hungry and singing birds.

Two gray squirrels stare at me as I eat breakfast, hoping I'll have pity and leave something for them. Especially since I have successfully ended their raids on my bird feeder. I doubt they'll starve with all the seedpods around the property but I have spoiled them a little through the winter with bread crusts and cookie crumbles.

Moving in the summer gave me a feeling of total privacy since I could not see any other houses except from the front door entrance. Then suddenly one night when I turned out the lights I was shocked to see many lights shining from neighboring houses beyond the tree area. It felt like the shades had all been raised and the world could see me, which wasn't really possible since I am on a cliff, but I never saw the other houses before.

As the winter continued, the lights became a comforting part of the view and in the daylight I could see the different occupants leaving for their business day or children for school. Even the family pets could be seen on their daily walks. Still I long now for the leafing of my privacy to return.

The winds are reported silently by the swaying of the treetops. The rains are heralded by the droplets splashing on the skylights. The snows quietly blanket the trees and buildings making everything spotless.

The activities of the school children echo above the trees. Cheers or football practice grunting can be heard some days, while other days the air is filled with the practicing of the marching band. I can track the improvement through the season.

It does make the year interesting as I observe the changes of all the seasons.

Common Sense

Do you have a reasonable quotient of common sense?

Being a survivor very often depends on common sense. It is basic, ordinary, practical judgment, but a lot of people either simply do not have their fair share or do not access it in times of stress.

I'm sure everyone would like to be a winner of a prize, whether a big one like the lottery, or a smaller one from a drawing of any variety. The lottery is a simple parting of your dollars at the lottery machine. Very often it only takes one trip to buy the ticket. Although somebody has to win, your chances are slim. Still you fantasize.

A second mode of being a winner can be as easy as answering your phone. This is where the use of common sense becomes very important. You may be told you have already won. What? Almost anything—car, house, trip or fortune, but you are told 'it's' yours now. Of course it sounds great! You want to claim your prize without delay. But now is the time to raise your caution antennae. You will be told someone is very anxious to deliver your prize. Sounds good so far, Just give your name, home address, a few small tidbits of information and then—your credit card number—whoa! The red lights should be flashing by now. Why, if you have won a free prize do you need to give out your personal credit card number? The explanation may be very swift and smooth and convincing, that since you are receiving such a valuable prize you shouldn't object to a little down payment of delivery fees or holding fees to secure your prize until the paper work can be completed. Sounds reasonable you think? Not so! If it is free as they said, it should cost you nothing! They called you; you didn't order anything from them.

If you sound reluctant, a second offer may be made. You can think about it and 'discuss' it for fifteen minutes and the call will be returned at which time a final decision is needed. If you sound reluctant, a second price may be offered, but only with great pressure for your decision and payment within minutes. The threat that you will lose this offer and someone else will receive it is geared to rush your decision

Red flags should be permanently waving in front of your eyes by now. If you cannot have time to consider and call back, it could be to prevent you from checking with the Better Business Bureau.

Whenever an offer sounds too good to be true, it probably is not a good offer. Practicing good common sense and being a survivor work hand in hand.

1. Be alert-resist offers too good to be true.
2. Never offer credit information to strangers.
3. Never give credit card numbers over phones unless you initiate the call.
4. Never pay up front for a "free" offer.
5. Guard yourself from areas of danger.
6. Resist areas of temptation or weakness: Ex.-alcoholism, peer pressure to smoke/drugs/joy-ride or computer chat-rooms of questionable moral value.
7. No challenge is too hard to meet if your will is to overcome it.
8. Any glimmer of eventual rescue or hope should be reached for and attempted in a situation of danger.
9. See your cup half-full.
10. Prayer, deep and sincere should be used for guidance when in doubt.

Greed often is never satisfied. Silver wants gold, gold wants platinum; small profit wants larger profit; hard work usually wants less work; long hour days desire same benefits with less hours or less effort.

I'm sure it is easier to be "born with it", but success is attainable and builds character when it is approached with honesty and integrity. It is far more rewarding to be able to see that face in the mirror each morning if it belongs to an honest and fair-minded person who conducts his life ethically and with compassion.

The Wounded People

Are not all of us wounded in some way—some physically, some lonely, some discouraged, some feeling less than adequate to face the daily schedule of life? Why then do we not reach out to each other to strengthen the weak threads and build a web, much like a spider's web, to support the weakened areas, by closing the empty gaps that cannot support the heavy burdens each person shares.

Much study has been made to investigate the merit of group support, and the findings are fascinating. Where some persons have been ready to give up completely, by finding others in similar circumstances and sharing experiences, under proper direction, they have found new reason to persevere and look forward even for a short term in the future. Doctors and psychologists are amazed at the results achieved when people who are total strangers, meet together on a regular basis and bond with similar experiences happening in their lives. Many are terminally ill but have many unresolved areas in their lives that remain undiscussed, even with family members, because they don't wish to burden their caregivers with their fears and discomforts.

On the surface they appear to be handling their 'problem' or 'illness' with ease and bravado, but alone at night, they retreat late into an area of abandonment. Feeling no one cares how they really feel so they must bear the fear alone.

Loving sons and daughters or friends are often hurting because they feel shut-off from a person they care for deeply. They often do not attempt to vocalize their concerns fearing they will upset the person that is ill or hurting.

Support groups are filling the gap for these necessary bonding friendships, as people feel free to discuss their true areas of concern without risk of hurt feelings. The need to vocalize their own concerns is essential in the steps of accepting their illness of situation so they can move to the next step of healing and set aside fears or worries. Often the opportunity to express love or true feelings to family members is postponed and the occasion does not return again. The family member may never hear how much they are loved and appreciated.

If you see yourself or one you love in this scenario, contact a group support program in your area. Hospitals or other health facilities and church offices can usually direct you to the proper group for your need. Don't wait to say what's in your heart. Don't wait until next week to do it. It may lift a heavy burden and replace it with a calming of the spirit, which can be, immeasurably beneficial.

The Sneak Attack

It's that quiet, insidious, unsuspecting, sometimes surprising, sneaky, vulnerable time of the year.

One day, sun is shining, temperatures are warm, and roads are dry. Next day, you wake to find that unmistakable soft white stuff covering the now pretty wet ground and when you step out the door to pick up the newspaper, you realize it's suddenly much colder than yesterday.

Likewise, one day you are feeling full of energy, checking over a full list of things to accomplish this holiday season. Time is carefully carved into a busy overstuffed schedule to achieve the impossible, only by the ultra optimist you are today—starting tomorrow.

Tomorrow dawns. Your head is spinning, your brain is pounding, even teeth hurt. You can't swallow and your vision is clouded. Your eyes are having difficulty even opening far enough to look at the clock, which is nagging you to get up with its curiously loud ticking that you never noticed before. You slowly move a perspiring semi-paralyzed arm to snuggle farther under the covers because this sweating body is suddenly freezing, when you discover something has somehow entered your bedroom on at least eighteen huge wheels and run over your bed with you still in it!

This can't be happening to me you think! It's all a horrible dream; I'll wake up any minute and get started on my busy day. You wait. You try to move that uncooperative arm once again. This time a shooting pain darts across your shoulders—you're sure now you've been run over and look around the area for the truck. It's gone already—hit and run!

You try to call for someone to help you and discover your voice has deserted you for a croaking frog sound.

You're not alone! Unfortunately many others are facing this miserable state of health every day, as the non-discriminating virulent flu germs travel around New Jersey. The empty thought enters your mind that it's probably too late to get a flu shot—you're right!

If you are lucky enough to have a friend or companion to empathize with your misery, you may be able to roll over and ignore the world for a few days until life enters your body again. Some aching bodies don't have that so-called luxury and will be dragging their weary bones, trying to keep some reasonable order in their lives and households until it becomes impossible to do so, and will have to give in to the inevitable.

So if it hasn't visited your house yet, pick up a few extra cans of soup and bottles of juice and a couple of magazines so you will not be completely without supplies when the sneak attack occurs.

Of course, if you are the ultimate optimist—it may skip over you and you could offer the soup and juice to a friend who wasn't as lucky as you. You might even want to buy a lottery ticket that day!

Center Stage

I was the center of attention at one point in my life. The world revolved around me, at least for a short time. It was a powerful position. One utterance from my lungs brought at least one worried face to my location. Sometimes as little as a cough or sneeze could evoke that same concerned look.

Years later, I was the concerned face looking down on the occupant of the power seat. The dimpled, smiling face that stared back was very pleased to have caused this attention. It didn't take her long to put cause and effect together and get satisfying results.

Once again, time has elapsed and the scenario is being replayed in the form of grandchildren. I have fortunately played both roles—cause of anxiety and receiver of anxiety. I understand cause and effect so much better now. In fact, I can observe it calmly with a silent grin. I even encourage a repeat scene and see the little wheels of memory and learning in progress.

When my children were little, I didn't realize so much learning occurred at such an early age. Little minds connect nerve synapses with each event that happens to them.

I remember being told, "You'll learn that when you go to school". Today you are almost certainly destined to failure if you're not enrolled in pre-school by age three. Formal learning techniques are incorporated with play and standards are set for a level of efficiency in pre-school.

In my early years, I did not have access to television or of course VCR's but my children grew up with such programs as Sesame Street, Mr. Roger's Neighborhood and Walt Disney. My grandchildren, keeping up with the present generation are enrolled in pre-schools before they are three years old.

My children learned many things at home although in a different manner. Counting started on fingers and toes, letters by playing blocks and repeating familiar letters as they learned the names of objects. Their social manners were learned and practiced by inviting friends to play and have lunch with them. Nutrition entered by helping prepare salads and small crustless sandwiches and of course pudding! Small muscles developed by manipulating homemade clay into objects and figures. Stories they had heard many times would be 'read' to younger siblings by following the pictures. Music was danced to and songs were memorized in play. Simple responsibilities were learned by helping with household chores.

We shopped together in the grocery store and learned to identify many items on the shelves and helped to count money for the clerk. Some things were made into games as well as jobs, like helping wash windows using a squirt gun or water pistol to do the job. Gardening was learned by planting seeds or small plants in window box gardens, helping them grow by watering and weeding.

Learning as well as teaching is universal and there is a wide variety of ways to achieve results. Each generation tries to improve in the methods, but the learning continues.

Growing up and Taking Blame

To you and the thousands of other parents who are miserable because of 'what you have done' to your children, I say this: Stop beating yourselves up! You did the best you could with the tools at hand, inexperience, clay feet, and the works.

No one knows why some children turn out to be champions in spite of parents who provided precious little emotional nourishment, while other kids, loved, wanted, tenderly nurtured, with all the so-called advantages, turn out hostile, irresponsible, unmotivated and unreachable.

I have come to believe in the genetic factor that has been ignored by many behavioral 'experts'. We all inherit our nervous system, and if the nervous system is fragile, it places severe limits on what a person can tolerate. Certain individuals are born survivors. They can withstand life's toughest blows and emerge the stronger for it. Others crumble in the face of minor adversity. The same fire that melts butter can make steel strong.

Let us not overlook personal responsibility. I am sick of hearing children blame their parents for their messed-up lives. People with all sorts of handicaps can and do make it in this demanding and competitive world.

Enough of this 'You damaged me, now take care of me' nonsense. It's a cop-out. Parental guilt laid on by your kids is so thick you can cut it with a knife. It serves no purpose except to perpetuate financial and emotional dependence and create a climate of insecurity and ultimate failure. God helps those who help themselves.

Comparison

I was the child, he was the parent. I looked to him for the big answers. He had the wisdom of many years to advise me. It was comforting not to have to know the answer to everything and to have an excuse to make an occasional mistake.

But all that has changed in recent years. My father now looks to me with frightened, trusting eyes, waiting for my wisdom to emerge because it greatly concerns his life.

I am his only living relative and have been given the charge by him to make all his decisions, financial and personal according to my best judgment. It is an awesome responsibility when I consider one mistake can affect his life with such magnitude that it could be irreversible.

My father had a stroke several years ago and has had increasing dementia. His mental light no longer shines as brightly. Although I still respect his fatherly position in my life, it is impossible for him to make decisions that are vital to his well being. As his daughter, some of the choices I have had to make seem almost a betrayal of his trust.

It was all simpler when he was alert and his mind was sharp and he chose what he wanted to do or objected strongly if he did not want to do something. Years of being dominated by an opinionated spouse made his decision to give up control an easier transition for him. I had wanted him to be able to regain some control in his life after her death but failing mental acuity in his senior years made this next to impossible. He seemed even relieved to turn responsibility over to me.

Dementia has reduced my father's verbal skills, resulting in complete absence of meaningful conversation. A critical decision arose recently when a crisis in his health demanded a choice of a mid-thigh amputation of his leg or do nothing but wait for the end of his life. I chose the only decision humanly acceptable and he had the amputation. The surgery was very successful and he is stable, comfortable and recuperating with no obvious sign that he realizes what has happened to him. God has been merciful in dulling his mind. At ninety-one years old he may leave this world without ever having to know the decision I made for him. I love him and he trusts that love implicitly.

Sale-ing

Most any weekend in the country from April until October, you'll find a diverse group of people, mixed ages, from a variety of social backgrounds, some wearing their Saturday morning 'scrunge-best', traveling the roads.

They will be meandering among tables and an array of boxes for the ultimate treasure that was the chief motivation for getting up so early and joining the troop of scavengers to every garage sale.

The reasoning? "I don't really need anything, but you never know when you'll discover something you've really been searching for".

This nomadic group includes widows, widowers, recent retirees with time to squander, lonely individuals looking for friendship, antique buff, collectors and ambitious young bargain hunters, trying to furnish their homes with a necessary or even unique piece of furniture.

Garage sales surpass all age limits. Many sales now highlight small sections for youngsters to display their salable items. Sometimes they feature toys, books or a collection of cards. While other entrepreneurs will have cookies and drinks to sell to sale-goers. Several of the younger sellers have become creative in their display and list their prices prominently including discounts, if you 'buy more than one'.

Once the 'bug' bites, it's a delightful way to spend early morning hours on Fridays and Saturdays. If you become 'professional', you map your course through the maze around your neighborhood. One method is to start at the larger, multi-family sales, so you see more with less traveling. A second method of choice is picking only sales that list specific items such as household furniture or children's toys. Weaving your way through the maze, you may discover unlisted sales along your route.

The most intriguing sales are barn sales or moving sales. They have the most interesting mix.

If you have small children or grandchildren, your clothing budget can get a big stretch as sales display a large variety of sizes for both boys and girls, most in good condition, simply outgrown.

Grandparents get a bonus budget-stretcher if they need a collection of toys or play items for visiting 'grands'

An older custom in families was simply passing clothing and toys on to other family members, but younger parents have discovered garage sales are a way to collect some funds for newer clothing needs.

Whether you have a special need or are curious, try joining the weekend parades. You might enjoy the sport.

Treasure Seekers

Maybe it's instinct or a vital part of being female, but the word SALE always seems to draw me like a magnet. Especially magnetic is a GARAGE-SALE. Even when I haven't the slightest desire to buy anything I just have to go—after all, I never know when I'll stumble over a hidden treasure.

Having conducted several of these junktique extravaganzas, I'm always amazed at what 'sale-freaks' will buy. Some of my least valuable stuff, things my husband has been embarrassed to take money for, has turned out to be the item several people will claw and grab at and be disappointed when they lose possession. Even when they are not exactly sure what it is the fact that someone else wants it establishes its value of the moment.

Brand new articles of obvious value will sit unwanted. Somehow if it's being sold at a garage sale, the general feeling is, 'there must be something wrong with it', while an old jelly-glass with a chip could be sold four times.

The last 'final, never-again, why are we doing this' garage sale we had, happened to be the day after a freak spring snowstorm. Our breakfast was interrupted at 7:30 A.M. with a doorbell ringing. Someone claiming she didn't know we would start at 9 A.M. and couldn't she just take a peek before she went to work so she wouldn't miss out. Our firm resolve not to allow anyone in before 9 A.M. went right down the stairwell with me as I opened the garage door to her. My disposition improved enormously as she proceeded to buy about fifty-five dollars worth of 'stock'! By then, nine o'clock was only an hour away. Before the door could be closed again, cars were arriving in a steady stream and I was sure I married a prince when my husband brought me a hot cup of coffee as he came to join me and the swarming treasure hunters.

Some were curious lookers, stopping briefly on their trek through the maze –pattern of sales around the area that day, clutching their copy of the classified section. Others lingered, haggling for lower prices, claiming not to have enough money, then spending more than the amount they claimed they had.

My neighbors never fail to stop by to cheer us on and to nose through what we're trying to unload. Bemoaning how full their garages' are at home they begin to wheedle how they might bring their stuff over, as long as we're going to the trouble anyway.

Sales and sale-goers are consistent for several morning hours. By noon, only an occasional car stops depending on what prized items are situated close enough to the road to grab their attention as they are driving by. Prices are adjusted during mid-day hours and by 3 P.M. it's pretty much fact that it's all over but the clean-up/

When we figured we had heated the outdoors long enough that day and a sizeable dent had been made in our garage, we wearily closed the door. My husband suggested we shower and dress, take some of the proceeds and go out to dinner to celebrate being able to see the garage walls again. I knew then there was yet another reason I married that guy!

Get A Grip

You're running late! The power went off during the night and messed up your alarm clock so you overslept. Can't find the pants you plan to wear, are they still in the cleaners? Make a second choice. There's not enough milk for your cereal and coffee- -you'll have to stop at the coffee shop for breakfast. Where did you leave your shoes? No clean socks in the drawer! Where are the car keys? Is it your day for the car pool? Damn!

It's going to be a long day and it hasn't even started. You have three clients to see before noon and you still have to go over your presentation

Backing out of the driveway, you see the gas gauge on near empty. Another stop! At the end of the block you realize you forgot your briefcase, back home again, more time lost!

Finally you are on your way and stop to pick up your rider. Leaning on the horn, you check your watch and find you're running twenty minutes behind your usual schedule. Your rider comes out running and apologizing, but you're too busy getting up steam to listen to him. His power went off too, so he's not at his best temperament either.

You flip on the radio and hear a report of a truck accident on your route, so you make several turns to detour the trouble spot only to discover you weren't the only one with that clever idea. You wait, and wait some more, then push into line to get ahead of the sports car that hesitated a second too long and you didn't want to waste another minutc. Horns blast, words blurt out, brakes screech, but you feel you've won that point which seems more important right now than safety.

There seems to be much more traffic than usual but you don't blame yourself for starting later. They should give you preference of the road. They just don't realize that fact. Another car sneaks up on the right shoulder and gains about seven car lengths before it cuts back into your lane and now you're really challenged! You start cutting left, keeping one eye on the car that got ahead of you and hear more screeching as you narrowly miss the right side of another car you cut off.

What are you trying to achieve?? High blood pressure? That's a certainty. A dented fender? You almost got it that time. Superiority of the road? Fat chance, since there are enough other enraged drivers vying for that position during drive time. Is this really necessary? Are you getting there any faster? Will you get there at all? Not if you continue to charge down the highways like you are the only car on the road.

You are also not the only one on the road with a hot temper. If the power went off last night, there are probably many late drivers this morning trying to make up lost time. All are not experienced drivers and may not be able to control their cars when they are cut off suddenly. Some may be using another road hazard, a car phone, to explain why they are late and are not paying close attention to your tricky maneuvers.

Rage may vent with mere words or gestures or escalate to erratic driving. Recently extreme rage has extended to shooting the offender! Now, is it still worth it? Sure you're late, you're mad at yourself and maybe everyone in the world today, but STOP! Get a grip! This is only one day—don't make it your last! Take a breath, and while you're doing that, think about the consequences of your road behavior.

Chalk this day up as not one of your shining best, but plan how you will be hearing a variety of stories similar to your dilemma. Hopefully you can laugh about it at the coffee machine.

Taking your rage onto the highway is an ideal way to shorten your life and maybe someone else's. Shorten the time of your three appointments and maybe by lunchtime you'll have gained back some of your lost time. And don't forget to check that setting on the clock for tomorrow morning!

Reflections

The day comes for each of us. Usually unexpectedly. One day, everything is fine, then suddenly the phone rings. The person in your life that was always so vital and busy is now less than able to function well.

In a hospital setting, an acute ailment might be treated quickly and successfully, but one blood test or one x-ray may reveal problems unknown until now.

Such is the case with my mother. Just two weeks ago she was at the helm, barking orders like the captain she has always been, keeping the ship running according to her law. A sudden infection brought her to a standstill and she was admitted to a hospital. Antibiotics were given. Blood tests were taken, CT scans and x-rays were accumulated. After several days, a once tranquil lifestyle was disrupted. A tumor was discovered, advancing rapidly. At the advanced age of 90 years, the options are sharply limited.

Mom has always been in control of her life and often everyone else's, so it was a devastating blow for her to have to take orders from someone else instead of giving them.

Within one week, there was a striking change in her health. Daily, pieces of equipment appeared in the room, until soon my father and I were picking our way carefully to get close to the bed without getting tangled in tubes and wires. Modern technology is wonderful, but can be frightening to family members when it is being used on their loved one. Most of the equipment is computerized and comes complete with sounds and voices.

My father felt his presence would aid in her recovery and emotionally, that cannot be discounted. But as the days continued, all the presence and loving compassion he could muster was not enough to pull off a cure. Every morning, he positioned himself at her bedside and only firm coaxing could pull him away with the promise of lunch. Clever suggestions to detain him at home were necessary to enable him to nap or rest. The emotional strain was also taking its toll on the stronger, healthier mate. Sleepless nights, constant worry and a denial of the seriousness of my mother's illness were all contributing to his fatigue.

As days turned into weeks, my mother's health continued to fail and some difficult decisions had to be made for her continuing care. Some of those decisions that none of us want to be asked to make. D.N.R. forms were signed to insure the prohibiting of aggressive intervention to prolong life beyond reasonable treatment. The doctor had assured us recovery was unlikely and death was only days away.

All nourishment was intravenous, veins were fragile and sites were becoming difficult to maintain. A morphine drip was established and my mother found the first steady comfort in many days.

My father's vigil remained daily, murmuring prayers with the determined thought she would overcome this hurdle as all others had been overcome in her life. But eventually, even his determination would not prolong her life. She slipped into a coma one morning early and died that afternoon.   His world was shattered. His mate of so many years was gone. He was alone. The tears of grief ran copiously and I felt almost helpless beside him. I had only seen him cry once before, when his mother had died.

Time and family support has brought him to his present place, which is comfortable and friendly. He has moved from his southern home to my northern state. Closer to family, he is making new friends slowly and beginning to relax in his new surroundings.

Every ending allows for a new beginning. Perhaps at his advanced years there is still time for a new beginning for him. Nothing in his life will ever be quite the same.

Many days and nights have empty spaces, but every day we try to plan some special event or change of scenery to give him a new perspective. Great-grandchildren have been able to gladden his heart since they live nearby and can manage to bring a smile to his face. Our goal is to convince him he is still important to the rest of his family and give him a reason for greeting each with the possibility of something interesting occurring to bring gladness once again to his heart.

Slug-Out

Sammy's his name, destruction's his game.

He looks so small and harmless. Almost like a fat midget worm, with feet.

But Sammy chomps his way through your gardens at night when no one can
  see him.

When the sun rises in the morning he is nowhere to be found and neither are
  your plants!

Maybe a stem here and there, and not much of that either.

Sammy's diet is luscious green leaves and fat juicy flower buds.

His sharp teeth chomp on the tender shoots until nothing is left but a stump,
  where a healthy blossoming plant used to be.

Any sensible gardener would search the garden centers to find the cure for
  this insatiable critter.

I searched, and finally found some wonderful pellets that promised me relief
  from this dilemma.

All I had to do was sprinkle them around my once beautiful absent flowers
  and add water. I did. I waited patiently. My reward was the reappearance of bright green leaves and eventually, luscious buds.

  Alongside, lay fat, once juicy slugs lying on their backs with their many legs curled under their puffed stomachs.

Problem solved, slugs gone. Now I can enjoy the fruits of my labors and admire my once-again flowered garden.

Open Door

One of the biggest steps out of childhood is that first day at school or pre-school. Seeing so many strange new faces you've never seen before can be pretty scary to a child. Today there are organized playgroups for 'only' children or children who live in suburban or rural areas. Learning to relinquish "mine" to another child when they are told to share is difficult for some children to learn.

Frequently the newcomer has enjoyed being king or queen at home, dictating to his parents in his own distinctive way what he or she will or won't do. One of the goals of group-play is cooperative sharing and "making nice", when an unexpected push or shove arises. Parents want their children to share without fighting, but Junior may not want to surrender without a battle.

It's humorous to watch anti-social non-sharers, trying to protect their turf when a larger or more aggressive child thinks otherwise. It can equal a 'survival of the fittest' in the animal kingdom.

There will always be dominant children in the world, and this is good—it's where tomorrow's leaders are born. There will also be less dominant children, who may be content to be followers. Watching children at play, you can usually pick out which ones are which.

At a playground, the secure or self –confident child will not be timid about climbing high or climbing a ladder to a slide. That child has been nurtured to be self –dependent at an early age. Other less confidant children may be frightened of height or reticent to claim a swing (for him) allowing himself to be pushed aside. He misses out on the fun of play and the joys of new friendships.

Pre-schools will nurture independence and confidence through teaching social graces and group discipline. Some teachers are born to this vocation. Others should seek different employ. Your child will be very lucky indeed if he/she finds a teacher well qualified to be a surrogate mom in the parents' absence.

Researchers have proved that children are very able to learn many things before the traditional school age of five years old. With computers on the scene, pre-school may be a helpful edge on your child's educational venture, but when it is as personal as your child's well-being, great care should be taken when choosing the right school for each individual.

The Big Sleep

Some people equate autumn with a dying season even to a degree of mild depression. But have you noticed the paisley beauty of the hillsides around the town? Nature is shifting gears from the oppressive heat of summer to the crisp air of autumn surrounded by a blaze of glory in overnight splendor.

The recent rains have created great heaps of leaves on the ground. If you can overlook the anticipation of weary arms that rake them, take a moment to admire the unusual and magnificent colors and designs of the variety of leaves before you proceed to remove them.

Some clever crafters know the secrets of preserving them with the use of glycerin and water and fashion them on decorative wreaths with wire in order to enjoy them longer. They seek out the best of golds and crimsons for their project.

Autumn really is a time to prepare for a seasonal nap. A chance to rest and recoup its' energy and return again with new vigor in the spring. It's also a time to reflect on our own lives. Maybe we view it as another year older, but we could also take notice of accomplishments or growth in areas of our lives. It's easy to see how quickly grandchildren grow—even from week to week. Our own children grow so quickly sometimes we hardly make it to the clothing stores for larger sizes in time to meet the need.

Spring has a tendency to sneak up on us quietly overnight, but autumn often arrives with a blast of crisp air and burst of color.

How has your own life grown? A maturing, a graduation, a promotion in your job, a move to a new home, a marriage or a new family.

Take notice of the new growth that is taking place instead of dwelling on the adding of pounds or a layer of age. Look to growth in your emotional and spiritual life and keep looking forward—soon it will be spring again.

How It Was

It was so much bigger then--really it was--!

The thick green hedge was at least twelve feet high, hiding the enormous backyard completely from the street. When I peeked through the dense greenery, I could see a big empty lot where all the big kids played baseball. The cars from the neighboring areas would park along the edges in the evening and watch the excited players and cheer on their particular hero. I couldn't really <u>see</u> the game, but I could <u>hear</u> all the cheering and occasionally disappointed moans, when someone struck out or dropped the ball.

The green grass was ever so –thick and cool, and I could lie on my back and watch the puffy piles of fluffy white clouds as they floated across the sky. Sometimes, the large colorful butterflies would land on the wide thick leaves of the grape arbor. Walking under the arbor was fun—like being in a tunnel. It was a little bit dark, but you could always see the twinkle of the sun as it peeked through the few bare spots, and then shone brightly at the end so it wasn't really scary. The thick vines would be loaded down with heavy stems full of dark purple grapes. They were always so cool and juicy on a summer afternoon. They must have been there for a hundred years, at least all of <u>my</u> lifetime-- and it was always a good hiding place.

It was such a great yard—it had EVERYTHING! A swing in the big apple tree, a climbing tower with tires and a slide and then you would find yourself in a giant sandpile. There was a big umbrella tree in one corner that drooped all the way to the ground, and was the best house-playing spot—nobody could see you behind the thick leaves.

Many an adventurous day was spent in my grandmother's magnificent backyard. Some days there were giant jungle animals lurking behind the grape arbor and around the hedges. Or elephants grazing in the far corners. Other days, the big ocean ships would sail in the massive 'wading' ocean from a foreign port to a strange land with the worlds' largest purple grapes.

Oh, the wonderful mysteries of my private world, the exciting, wonderful world of my grandmother's backyard, interrupted only by an occasional welcome call from the edge of my world to 'come over here for a few minutes and see if the cookies are any good today'.

Mysterious, magical, and not-ever-quite forgotten days, but then, didn't everything seem that way when you were four years old!

Joey's Birdfeeders

Joey's favorite place was at the counter, sitting on the high stool by the window in front of his birdfeeder. It was his very own birdfeeder, his Mom and Dad had given it to him for his birthday, and he had helped his Dad hang it up in front of the kitchen window. It was a special kind that hung from a wire line, so the squirrels could not reach it.

Every morning Joey ate his bowl of cereal and his toast in front of his 'bird window'. He would sit very still, so the birds would not see him and fly away.

Joey and his Mom went to Mr. Johnson's feed store and bought special "Songbird" seed with lots of sunflower seeds because the littlest birds especially liked them. They had to fill his feeder every day; he had so many bird friends that visited it daily.

Early in the morning one red finch would come to the feeder to check out the food supply, then alert the others and soon there would be two in the feeder and three sitting on the wire waiting their turn.

One day Joey saw one little bird with a lame wing, eating on the ground. He saved some of his toast crumbs and his Mom gave him half a muffin to crumble for the little bird. Joey threw the crumbs on the ground then sat down on the steps to watch. The lame bird came near them and tasted one or two crumbs, then hopped away by the big spruce tree. Joey waited quietly and pretty soon the lame bird came hopping back and ate some more. That made Joey very happy.

Joey's Mom bought him a book with pictures of birds in it so he could tell the names of his dinner guests. He had many sparrows, and wrens, chickadees and finches, and sometimes a kinglet with his red cap. Joey knew his birdfeeder was special because sometimes he would have a titmouse with his pointed hat, or a mommy cardinal come to dinner. Usually the daddy cardinal was waiting on the ground to protect her. He was very important looking with his bright scarlet feathers and pointed hat. Joey thought his face looked like the Lone Ranger's mask.

Sometimes Joey would draw a picture of some of the birds and take them to school to show to his teacher and classmates. His teacher would let Joey talk about his birdfeeder and tell his classmates about his feathered friends. That always made Joey feel very important.

Pogo's Lesson

One day Jimmy's Dad brought home a puppy. It was black with white spots on it. One white spot was right around his left eye.

It was a frisky pup. He liked to run and would sometimes fall down because he would get so tired.

When he was excited he would jump up and down, so Jimmy decided to call him Pogo, because it made him think of a Pogo Stick.

Jimmy fed him every day and took him for walks on his new leash. All the neighbors liked Pogo because he was friendly.

When Pogo played in the backyard with Jimmy he did not need his leash, because Jimmy watched him carefully.

Jimmy and Pogo were playing ball one day and just as Jimmy ran after the ball so he could throw it again, Pogo ran around the side of the house and very soon he was in the street in front of the house.

Jimmy looked and looked for him and called his name, "Pogo, where are you? Pogo, here Pogo--" but still he could not find him. Then he heard brakes squealing and his little heart almost stopped beating. He thought Pogo had been hit by a car. Just as Jimmy's Mom came out of the house, a man walked toward them carrying Pogo. Pogo looked very frightened and was shaking in the man's arms.

"I'm so glad I saw your puppy in time and could stop my car quickly," he said. "He looked like he was very special to someone."

"Oh! He is!" said Jimmy, "He's my very own puppy! Thank you, mister. I will not let him get out of the yard again."

Jimmy's Mom thanked the man again as she handed Pogo back to Jimmy. "We are so lucky you are a careful driver."

Pogo was so frightened he was still shaking. Jimmy sat on the ground petting him and talking to him for a long time and soon Pogo was happy again and jumping up and down all over the backyard. He knew the big street was not the place for him ever again!

The Storm

Silently it fell during the night, sneaky and quiet. That's what it usually does. Then in the morning, when you look out the window, there it lies, defiantly. This time, it was about four inches deep and still snowing heavily.

The media had warned of this storm, but they had predicted storms frequently in the past and they fizzled. It looked like they finally guessed right this time and it was falling at the rate of one and half inches per hour. The neighborhood responded in a variety of ways. Some were shoveling at the moment, some were peering out of their windows, and I—taking the only sensible reaction on a Saturday morning—decided to make coffee! Sometime after two cups and couple of eggs and toast, I located the shovel and gave it a respectable effort, but one hour later, it hardly looked touched.

The radio continually reported the progress of the year's worst blizzard and how dangerous it was to travel so stay home except for an emergency. Sounded good to me. I digested the morning paper, which somehow made it through the storm, and watched the progress through the family room window. One thing was a fact; I'd wasted my time shoveling.

Traffic was non-existent, not even a plow. The only moving bodies were those of necessity, walking their dogs.

Somewhere during the early afternoon hours, a sudden dark shadow passed the windows in the room. I could not believe what I saw. What used to be a regally standing sixty –foot blue spruce tree, in my neighbors yard, was now lying down ever so still and quiet in the middle of my back yard –taking up the entire yard, with it's roots pulled out of it's former location. Didn't even brush my house, just quietly fell over. It was home to perhaps a hundred birds, who were also so surprised; they were still in it!

At least thirty minutes later, they gradually flew from the tree, a few at a time and visited my several feeders, then returned to the tree, but seemed unsure of how to sit on it. Their vertical home had become horizontal. Cardinals, titmice, wrens, junkos, phoebes and finches, all equally disoriented. Guess they were going to have to check out new real estate for their future home.

Me—A Grandmother!

Never anxious, I assumed it was a likely possibility, since I was a mother of three. Our eldest son, married several years, with no signs of impending parenthood did not disturb me. They were struggling to achieve their chosen lifestyle, attending school and filling every space in their busy daytimers. I told them, don't have grandchildren just to please me, do it for yourselves—no pressure.

My daughter told me if I was waiting for her, I should 'rent a kid', so I didn't think I should hold my breath for her either.

Then, a sudden phone call from child number three one evening gave me a different perspective. After general greetings, I reported the arrival of a cousin's new baby.

"Guess we're next," he said.

It stopped me cold! Married not quite a year, I knew they had not planned for a family yet, but that's when most babies make their first appearances, earlier than expected. When I regained my ability to speak, I bubbled my enthusiastic approval of his news. He quickly turned the phone over to his bride.

"We're awfully surprised," she said.

"First babies are usually that way, I'm so happy for you."

"You're not upset that we didn't wait longer?"

"Not one bit! I'm putting in my application as baby-sitter, am I accepted? One thing though, when I return this little darlin' be assured it will be spoiled rotten. That's my job as grandma."

"That'll be fine with us, we're going to want someone to show us how it's done along with a lot of other things we don't know on this subject yet."

"Can I tell the world yet?" I asked.

"Sure, I guess so. We got the official word today—I think the world should know. I can't believe it yet myself."

It sure is a leap of faith, but in seven and a half months, when I hold this miracle in my arms we'll still find it hard to believe.

<u>STORIES</u>

The Fisherman

" Please Mom, can I? When I catch one, you can eat it too."

Billy's pleading whine came from extensive practice. He wanted to go fishing so-o-o badly! Why wouldn't Mom take him? A couple of times she told him she was too busy and when he asked this time, she said, 'we'll see'.

Now Mom's 'we'll see' was not to be taken lightly. It didn't necessarily mean 'yes', but then again, it wasn't a definite 'no' either. Sometimes it depended on just how she said it. If it was drawn out and slow, you might as well forget it – it's closer to 'no'. But, if she said it quickly, then you had a pretty good chance for a 'yes'. It was a 'quick one' today.

The truth was, that Mom wasn't much of a fisherman, but a first-grader wasn't old enough to figure that out by himself yet.

For two days Billy had worked on her, trying to worm a promise out of her. She never broke a promise to him! He even brought her a fistful of pansies from the neighbors' garden to weaken her, but no promise yet. Finally, in desperation, he pestered Dad after work one night. When Dad was tired, he would most likely say yes to anything, but then Mom had to get him to keep his promises.

"Okay Bill," Dad said wearily, "you dig enough worms and I'll take you fishing tomorrow morning."

"Oh boy, Dad! How many worms 'ya want? Huh Dad? How many do I hafta'dig up?"

"Oh, I guess about five will be enough."

"O.K. – Hey Mom, can I go out after supper? It won't be for long, but I gotta' get some worms."

"We'll see Billy," she said quickly, "now up to the table for dinner."

"Sure, Mom." That was 'yes' for sure, he thought.

Dinner disappeared in a hurry that night from Billy's plate. Even the potatoes that usually got pushed all around the plate until it looked like he'd eaten most of them simply because the little mound was spread out.

"May I be excused, Mom?" He asked eagerly.

"How about dessert, Billy?"

"No thanks Mom, I'm full."

"All right."

He scrambled away from the table, giving one quick swipe to his mouth with his napkin, "About the worms, Mom," he ventured.

"A half -hour, but that's all."

"Gee thanks, Mom. Can I take one of your coffee cups to put the worms in?"

"Absolutely not!" she shrieked. "There's an empty coffee tin on the back porch, use that."

The door slammed and Billy headed straight for the garden. He found a trowel and began digging, but progress was slow, as the ground was very dry. Two big fat worms scrambled around the hole and Billy tried to scoop them on his shovel, but they squirmed and wriggled and soon disappeared while Billy was still figuring out how to get them into the can without touching them.

His mother came out the door after about twenty minutes and called, "How many did you get, Bill?"

"I've got a half –one already Mom, wanna' see it?"

"Ick! – Not really." She got Dad's fork from the cellar and dug up a small section in the garden.

"Golly Mom, that's super! Look at that big one – would you put 'em in the can for me?"

"You're the fisherman, Bill, if you want them, YOU get them into the can."

He tried the trowel, then he tried two sticks and finally by turning the can on the side, he pushed some in with the sticks. It was a lengthy process because some were busy crawling out of the can, while Billy was pushing others in. By the time it was 'dark enough' according to Mom, he had seven and a half worms.

"Think that's enough, Mom?"

"I think so, Daddy said about five didn't he?"

"I'm gonna' put them under my bed until tomorrow morning."

His mother gasped – "The back porch is as far as they're going in THIS house young man! And please go in quietly, Daddy's sleeping on the couch."

Too early the next morning, a persistent finger was poking Mom on her arm. She opened one eye with great effort and saw a freckled face with two huge eyes staring at her.

"Is it time yet, Mom?" asked Billy.

"If you wake up your father this early, he'll never take you fishing! Now get back in your bed until I call you," she whispered loudly. "The fish aren't even awake yet."

Billy was dejected, but returned to his room slowly. He stopped in the bathroom for a drink of water. Then he tiptoed out to check on his worms – too dark to see them. Guess I might as well go back to bed, he thought.

After many trips to check to see if Daddy's eyes were open and several drinks of water later, Mommy called, "Billy, you can start getting dressed if you want to now."

If I want to – Wow! He was dressed before Mom was even out of bed.

"I'll set the table for breakfast Mom, okay?"

"Wonders will never cease! Okay, I'll be right there."

Breakfast seemed to take forever to Billy, but finally he and Dad were on their way to the river with a fishing pole and his can of worms.

Billy chattered excitedly, "What'll we put our fish in when we catch it, Dad?"

"Let's catch it first, Bill. Then you can carry it home, I'll show you how."

"What kind will we get – scallops?"

His dad laughed. "No Bill, not scallops. We'll take home whatever kind likes your worms. Here we are, this looks like a good spot. Get out a worm, Bill."

"They're gone, Dad! --I don't see any!"

"Dump the can over."

He did, and there they all were on the bottom of the can.

"Put one on this hook, Bill."

"I can't Daddy – they wiggle too much!"

"Well, if you're going to come fishing, that's the first thing you'll have to learn to do. Just pick it up in your fingers."

He tried – REALLY tried, but the worm would curl around his finger and he'd drop it. He tried holding it in his palm, but it tickled his hand so he had to drop it again and rub his palm on his dungarees to scratch it. His big blue eyes were pleading for Dad to help him out, but dad's face looked very serious as he'd say, "Try 'er again, son."

Billy was afraid to pinch the worm and he was afraid the worm would be hurt if it were stuck on the fishhook. After much trial and error, the worm was almost on the hook and Billy was grateful for Dad's push of his thumb to catch the worm on tight. He was beginning to taste his breakfast again by now.

By the time the worm was in the water, Billy was beginning to wonder if he really wanted to fish. What if that worm falls off? I'll have to do another one! He swished the pole up and down the river half –heartedly and was very disappointed that the fish didn't leap out of the water to get his worm after all the trouble he went to just to get it on there.

After what seemed a long time to him, Billy said, "Dad; I don't think the fish are very hungry today, maybe we –Oh gosh!" He saw the cork bob – "Hey Dad, I got one! Look!" With a big yank, he pulled on the pole making a sweeping ark with the line, followed by a five and one-half inch trout, which came flying past Dad's face and flopped to the grass. From the first yank, Billy began running up the embankment of the river pulling his pole with him, the 'prize catch' flopping along the grass.

His dad began to holler to him, then suddenly burst out laughing, as if remembering his first fish.

Billy was still running with his fish flopping behind him when he became suddenly conscious of Dad calling his name. He stopped, dropped the pole and scurried to rescue his treasure. It was wiggling desperately on the end of the hook as he picked it up to look at it closer; not stopping for a moment to think that it was wiggling twice as much as the worm that enticed it. Let's take it home to show Mom, dad. It's big isn't it?" His eyes were beaming proudly.

Dad took an appraising look, smiled and answered, "Sure is, Bill, it's big enough for us."

Dad helped Billy unhook the fish and he strutted proudly toward home carrying it with his index finger stuck in the gills, leaving Dad to gather up the pole and worms. Billy could think of nothing except his 'prize catch'.

It was years later, that Dad confessed to Billy, he really considered throwing it back because it was under-sized, but thought it was easier to pay the contemplated fine than face his son's disappointment.

First Day in Kindergarten

It's Jimmy's first day in kindergarten. This is a giant step in his world. Sure, he's been to pre-school, but now he was going to REAL school, and he was ready, couldn't wait!

Exciting days, preceded his big day. Some things he didn't think were much fun. A doctor's visit for a booster shot and a dentist's visit for a cavity check – but the mall for new sneakers and some schoolboy clothes and a new lunch box was a much happier outing. His lunch box had a cold pack for his juice. A new backpack and a slicker for the rainy days were next.

Two days before opening day, the school invited Jimmy and Mommy to meet his new teacher. He visited his homeroom, saw his desk and all the neat things he would play and learn with. Bright colors, and big windows made the room very cheerful. He saw 'his' playground with swings and jungle gym and activity toys. His big blue eyes were darting all over, trying to take in everything at once.

Jimmy lived near the school and there was a college campus in the middle of a straight path he could take to his school. Mommy took him on the college path to get him accustomed to his route, pointing to landmarks as they walked. They passed a house that had a big dog. It was wearing a chain leading to its' doghouse and was sleeping.

When daddy got home that night there was lots to tell him. One thing Jimmy didn't know was his daddy had walked this same path, passed another large dog and sat in the same classroom when he was 5 years old.

The big day came and Mommy walked him with his sister to the end of his kindergarten path. When he got to the end of the walkway he said, "Goodbye Mommy, you go home now!"

Mom's chest and throat got tight and she tried with all her might to hold back that tear that was ready to drop as her little boy took another big step to 'independence'. She gave him a hug and a kiss and again he said, "Go home now mommy!"

Several days passed and the teacher called Jimmy's mom to let her know he could travel on a mini-school bus if she approved. They had discussed this before, but she was unsure. Now when Jimmy heard about it, the decision was a very definite yes. Mommy was not able to convince him it was better to let her drive him once the vision of the big yellow school bus was in his mind.

Now after less than a week, he acts as if he had been going to school all his life. He jumps out of bed eagerly every morning, hurries to put on his schoolboy clothes and eats his breakfast quickly so he can sit on the porch steps to wait for his yellow bus.

Kindergarten has become a full day of school since it has been proven children learn at a much earlier age than educators had previously thought.

Jimmy has 'important' homework each night. Mommy helps him drill with his flash cards and Daddy helps him read a story for a book report. As he plays with his sister, she often repeats what he has learned about letters and numbers.

It is exciting to see his exuberance for school. Jimmy is motivated to exert himself since some subjects include class trips to a local farm to visit animals and see how vegetables grow.

His vocabulary is growing daily and conversations he has at home surprise his parents as he tells them about things they didn't know he knew. The door to the world has been opened to him and he is very anxious to find out what is behind it. Jimmy is growing up.

Holy Meatballs

It has been said, 'many hands make light work', but sometimes the theory that ' more is less' changes the logic and the whole effort results in disorder and confusion. Such was the case at a recent church dinner, conducted by the willing, eager volunteers, most of whom had never been privileged to even view from afar, the interior of a reasonably well-equipped restaurant kitchen.

Some were infused with an air of importance and authority with the very thought of being able to somewhat control the fate of sixty or seventy unsuspecting, hungry dinner guests. Others were feeling lost in the environs, but willing to fake some semblance of efficiency to bolster their confidence.

The menu happened to feature spaghetti and meatballs. Now spaghetti is a strange food—it appears to clone itself and become much more than you thought after it's cooked, much like a cup of rice, those little innocent grains that could feed the military in the battlefield. Two pounds of potatoes makes a nice heaping mound of mashed potatoes, while two pounds of spaghetti looks like it might feed the neighborhood. Maybe it has something to do with the fabulous sauce and meatballs, or the fact that spaghetti lovers are just crazy about their choice, but once that tangled mountain starts being served it seems to disappear suddenly.

During the busy serving time that evening, smiles took the place of expertise at times and generous portions more than pleased the hungry guests. When it appeared the big rush was almost over and the tangled miles of pasta had a definite dent in it, one exuberant chef thought we should cook 'just a little more' for any late arrivals and immediately, while the thought was still skimming around in the minds of the various helpers, emptied two full boxes of spaghetti into the massive cooking kettle .

The many diners seemed to enjoy the efforts of the chefs and having eaten all their stomachs' could hold, which turned out to be a considerable amount—fourteen pounds of spaghetti, about one hundred and fifty meatballs and the same amount of sausage, not to mention nine or ten loaves of bread and many gallons of mouth-watering tomato sauce that had been flavored superbly.

Most of the volunteers drifted away from the area of serving as soon as the line ended, perhaps fearing someone might say they didn't like it, though more than likely they would have heard kudos for the excellence of the sauce and the service. Whatever the reason, it must have appeared safer when the room was nearly empty.

The clean-up methods of attack varied. Some carried one plate in each hand to the kitchen, while some stacked cluttered, sloppy plates on top of each other leaving the resulting mess to be cleaned off in the kitchen from precariously staggered piles. One or two attacked with precision, working as a team, carefully scraping and stacking on trays to be presented to the delegated dish-washer of the night for rinsing before their final destination in the dishwasher.

Tradition predicted much of the action, when it was obvious there was a better, less labor-intensive method, but who was brave enough to tell the many eager gray-haired volunteers that they were doing it all wrong and your way was much better? Some might have been patient and submissive enough to listen to the new method, while others would be making a mental note to be much too busy at anything else, to be able to help at the next event.

In many of the quaint old churches, the time-honored traditional dinners continue, annually, bi-annually or even more often, and basically the same diligent group of seasoned and dedicated volunteers gather regularly, roll up their collective sleeves, and lend their smiles and exuberance to the success or failure of every dinner performed for the church's purposes.

Officers are nominated and elected, leaders are appointed and praised, but without the ever –present, seemingly anonymous volunteer, the work of the committees' choosing might never be accomplished.

The projects are completed, the reports are written up, the appointed leaders are dutifully accredited with the success of each milestone and perhaps a general thank-you to 'all-who-participated', but those who were there, sit quietly in the congregation, smiling to themselves, knowing that the purpose was achieved, they did their share, and the 'Great-leader' would know what they did to help—and that's what really mattered.

The Whirlwind

"Good-bye—Have a good time, see you Thursday."

Kathy closed the kitchen door quickly, before the children could glimpse Mommy and Daddy leaving. Glancing around at six active pre-schoolers tumbling on the floor in the family room, she began to wonder if she hadn't taken on more than she could handle. Well, too late now she sighed, there goes the car out the driveway—Chicago, here they come—and kids, well here you are!

What a week to have wall to wall kids—with John away, too. Her husband was on a business trip and would miss all this bedlam. "Lucky stiff," she thought aloud.

Gathering up pajamas and slippers from bedrooms and suitcases she summoned the little troop, "P. J. time, gang!"

Within five minutes, she knew it was the wrong approach. Six bare bottoms were on display in the middle of the kitchen, amid a mountain of unidentified underclothes, overalls, dresses and shoes.

"Kristy, are these your pajamas?"

"I dunno," came the reply.

"I think they're mine, Aunt Kathy," said a wee little voice.

After a quick measure, which proved she was right there was one down, five to go.

It was a hectic half-hour—two legs going into one pajama leg, tops going on backwards, clothes flying in every direction, shoes clunking, bumping, tickling and squeals of laughter, but somehow, everyone ended up with a top and a bottom. As Kathy gathered up the little mountain from the kitchen floor, she had to smile as she saw six little heads in a cluster in front of the TV watching Bugs Bunny.

Tomorrow, she thought, I'll take them two at a time instead of all at once.

Later that evening, every bed in the house had at least one little mound under the blankets with a tousled head poking out at the top and every other mouth was plugged with a tiny thumb.

Kathy awoke early every morning that week to gales of laughter and the pitter-patter of many pairs of feet reminding her it was time to dress and feed the natives.

After a squirming, wriggling noisy breakfast session, the mornings were filled with organizing play and passing out cookies between household chores and multiple trips to the ever-popular potty.

Lunchtime was an assembly line of peanut butter and jelly sandwiches, then peace and quiet for sometimes almost an hour and a half while the restless natives napped.

One particularly warm sunny morning, Kathy turned the children loose in the backyard with an assortment of carriages, bicycles and trucks and gave a sigh of relief to have the house empty for an hour. She was soon to find out it was a rash thought, because a steady stream of tiny taps began on the door asking for drinks of water, or cookies, drippy noses seeking tissues and once even a presentation of her prettiest pansies, complete with roots from the flower bed.

Once again, the children's' naptime revived Kathy for the 'evening banquet of the little people'

The week went by all too quickly, and just at dinnertime one evening, Jane and Bob came peeking into the kitchen door. The usual dinnertime performance was in full swing and Kathy didn't even notice them until she heard, "Got two more plates of that spaghetti for the weary travelers?"

"Oh c'mon in and join the institution," Kathy said.

The children squealed with delight when they saw Mommy and Daddy and dinner was forgotten for the moment while hugs and kisses were exchanged all around.

"Did'ja bring me somethin'?"

"I been a good girl, Daddy."

"Me too."

Kathy restrained a groan when she heard Kristy tell her mother she didn't want to go home and couldn't she stay longer!

When they were assured of future presents after suitcases were unpacked, they settled down to dinner and dishes of chocolate pudding and guesses about what their presents might be.

Kathy fixed hurried plates of spaghetti for Jane and Bob and during dinner they both talked at once trying to tell her all that had happened on their trip.

Later that evening, with her own three children tucked in for the night, Kathy sat in the quiet of the living room with a steaming cup of herbal tea. She thought about her three little visitors, who were now probably sleeping on the back seat of the car, wending its' way back to Baltimore. Jane and Bob had had a wonderful whirlwind of a week among business celebrities and nightclub circles, and she— yes, she had a whirlwind week too. Of a different kind, to be sure, but one with memories which would linger long after Jane and Bob had forgotten the nightclubs, and the children themselves would probably have forgotten their visit. She flipped on the television and settled herself in her favorite chair for an evening of satisfying and well-earned quiet. She had to admit to herself she was glad there were only three mounds sleeping upstairs. John had better not bring up that idea he had of 'another little one in the house' or he might be asked to change his address! If the vote were to be hers, this would remain a 'three-mound' household.

The Tenants

Once in a while something unique happens in your private corner of the country that delights your soul and sparks you with hope and enthusiasm for life. It has happened to me, just two feet outside my kitchen window.

I'm an avid birdwatcher. I tend my feeders faithfully year round. It probably has spoiled the feathered life in my neighborhood. They could find food in the summer, with a little more effort, while depending on the feeder system for the winter. But I like seeing and talking to them, while they chirp and chatter back to me. It is because of my year-round tending that a family of finches, checking out real estate for a nesting site, decided on my hanging bird feeder to build their nest.

Refilling the feeder one-day, I discovered several twigs and leaves in the feeder and quickly scooped them out with the empty hulls of seed. The very next day there was a substantial amount of twig and grass debris once again in the feeder. After observing a short while, the carrier was revealed. She was a very plain-feathered house finch. Diligently she carried and weaned the twigs and grasses all day. By evening the basics of a nest were constructed over a bed of about three inches of wild birdseed mixed with sunflower seeds. Several more days the would-be mother continued to weave and build. Papa finch, a bright splash of red on his head and breast, could be seen checking the progress and visiting the nesting site occasionally.

Three days passed. Mama finch, now nicknamed, 'Plain Jane', took up residency and within two days, one egg was nestled in the new home. I watched carefully from my kitchen window, moving slowly in that area so she wouldn't be disturbed. Each day a new egg was added until soon there were five in the nest.

Mama finch was in constant attendance unless startled away or feeding. Papa finch would sometimes visit on the edge of the nest and other times sit on the edge of the roof to observe and guard the nest.

I carefully checked my bird books and found the incubation period was 12-16 days. The hatched young would then be confined in the nest for another 11-19 days.

Early on a Friday morning, 'Jane' had a visitor at her nest. Papa had come to admire the first of her brood, which hatched during the night. The baby hatchling, the tiniest fluff of feathers I'd ever seen, was fluttering in the nest.

There was much activity in the nest that day. Papa visited frequently, bringing food to 'Jane'. She reached up to his mouth and took it eagerly then jumped to the side of the nest and fed it directly into the baby's mouth. After the feeding, mama resumed her position on the nest to keep the baby and remaining eggs warm.

Early next morning I was anxious to see what progress occurred. More flurry of feathers and chattering of a busy mama and papa. They were tending more tiny gaping mouths suspended on wobbly necks, peeping and stretching for food. Papa was proving to be a 'Dad of the '90's', busily carrying his full share of the feeding duties. Mama was stuffing tiny beaks on one side of the nest and Papa stuffing others on the opposite side, almost overwhelmed by their new duties.

Throughout the day, several feeding frenzies were staged. In between there was peaceful quiet in the nest with a pile of fluff only rising and falling to the rhythm of breathing while Mama flew in search of food for herself.

Neighbors came to peer into the nest from inside my kitchen window. All were more than willing to use the front door to avoid disturbing the new parents whose nest was next to the back door. Our consensus counted a population of four chicks. Each day showed subtle change.

The feathers became larger and the babies grew larger and stronger.

The appearance of the once tidy nest had changed dramatically. Since the arrival of four new tenants, who were in various stages of potty training, the nest was now unsightly and sloppy. Each baby in turn hoisted his or her rear to the edge of the feeder and let nature take over their bodily functions, right down the curved exterior of the feeder. It didn't take too many of these 'duty' calls to make the exterior a disgusting mess. As the days went by, even my neighbors cringed when they took their daily progress peeks.

After watching carefully for many days, I had to be away from my home for several days and when I returned I was surprised to find the nest empty. I observed discreetly for two more days and saw 'Jane' return several times, perch on the edge a moment and fly away. Assuming the family had vacated. I removed the feeder, emptied and scrubbed it among many large swallows and cringing expressions on my face, then refilled it with fresh sunflower mix and rehung it. Within two hours, two brightly colored young males and one young female were busily feeding in their cleaned ex-nest.

During the following month I was treated to early morning chirps and magnificent trills of song from my bird family as they confidently visited and ate their fill daily. Then one morning in early July, it was like de'ja vu as I filled the feeder with seed and noticed once again, bits of branch and twigs being gathered in the feeder. Apparently my satisfied tenants are gracing our rental facilities for another term of family tending.

The Neighbor

"I just don't like her, Jack, she's kind of uppity. She's not like us," Sally said.

"She's not so bad, Sal, why don't you give her a chance. She doesn't know too many people," defended her husband.

"Leave it to a man to stick up for a blonde," Sally retorted.

"Worried?" He chided.

"That'll be the day!"

Marcia and her husband had bought the Lesley house next door about a month ago. Sally had been very friendly with old Mrs. Lesley until she died a year ago.

Just what was it about Marcia Evans that she didn't like, Sally wondered? Her hairdo? Who else wears a French twist everyday? That Boston accent? Maybe-or was it envy? Marcia was always perfectly groomed, never appeared rushed. She had plenty of time to pursue her pastime of painting. That was something Sally rarely had-spare time. And Marcia was seemingly content not to indulge in petty gossip, at least not the local coffee klatch. She was different all right.

Sally and Jack had lived in the community about five years. Jack commuted each day to a small advertising firm in the city where he was employed as a junior executive. Their only child, Jimmy, had been almost three years old when they moved here, now he was a second grader. He was a redhead with a half million freckles around a pug nose.

Weeks would go by when Sally would hardly think about Marcia. She was busy with her social-suburban activities—PTA president, homeroom mother for Jimmy's second grade class, woman's club treasurer, hospital volunteer aide once a week and of course the regular coffee-klatching to keep up with the intimate local happenings.

Marcia Evans always seemed to slip into the conversation. She graduated from school with Carol Carson's cousin, so she couldn't possible be older than 26-six years younger than Sally, something she felt she mustn't let Jack find out. Occasionally she'd catch a glimpse of Marcia in her yard sunning herself and would purposely be too busy to wave.

Jack, on the other hand, seemed to take every opportunity to wave if he saw Marcia in her yard or holler a very neighborly hello and Sally thought he did it purposely to make her bristle, but she would force herself not to comment. Sally ran into Marcia one morning in the supermarket. Try as she would to avoid her, eventually she came face to face with her coming up the same aisle.

Hello, Mrs. Harrison, I was planning on calling you this afternoon. A Mrs. Johnson called and asked me to solicit our block for the Hospital Fund and I wanted to ask you how to go about it. She said you were the chairlady last year. I've never done anything like this before in my life. Would you help me?"

Sally was taken off guard completely. Here she was put on a spot by someone she didn't want to like, but didn't know why. She didn't want to help her and she didn't want her friendship. How can you dislike a person when she was being friendly?

"Oh—I—well—sure, I guess so"

Sally could have kicked herself—why didn't she just say no!

"I'd really appreciate that," Marcia went on, "would you let me know when is a convenient time to come over or would you rather come to my house? I'd love to have you."

"I'm free this afternoon," Sally heard herself saying, "I could come over about two o'clock if that's alright. Jimmy will be at his grandmother's house."

"Oh, thank you so much—are you sure I'm not inconveniencing you?"

When Sally assured her she wasn't she thanked her again profusely and continued with her shopping.

What did I get myself into, Sally thought. Sucker Sal—well, I've got to go through with it. How dumb can you be—doesn't even know how to collect money!

Later that day, Sally found herself standing on Marcia's back porch. She purposely avoided the front door so her neighbors might not see her and suppose she was being friendly.

Marcia opened the screen door before Sally could knock, "Do come in Mrs. Harrison, I saw you coming up the walk. I have some Kool-Aid fixed for us, would you like some?"

Sally said yes and noticed that Marcia had set a cozy table with a blue and white luncheon cloth and tall thin frosted glasses on saucers. There was a plate with homemade cookies in the center of the table next to a blue bud vase with a single rose.

Marcia proceeded to tell Sally every detail of information she knew about Mrs. Johnson's conversation, which was mostly unimportant. The thought flashed through Sally's mind that this was a ruse to get her over for a visit, but she dismissed it quickly. After all, how could someone want you for a friend when you were making it so clear you didn't want her friendship?

"I admire your son, Mrs. Harrison."

"Please call me Sally."

"All right—I see him playing outside often. He's going to be a handsome young man."

124

"What —oh—yes—thank you. Sally had been so preoccupied admiring the colonial decoration of Marcia's house, that she hardly knew who Marcia was talking about. "He looks like his father," she said, "now about this soliciting, there really isn't much to it. Just knock on their doors and ask if they care to contribute and give them a receipt. If they aren't home, I'd just leave the literature and envelope in the mailbox"

"It sounds easy enough, I just get nervous meeting new people. Would you like to see some more of the house?"

"Oh, I don't want to bother you, Marcia," although she was dying to see it <u>all!</u>

Marcia led the way through one very smartly decorated room after another. Sally had to admit to herself, this girl certainly had a flair for interior decoration.

Later, when Sally entered her own living room, she thought, well, she can afford it, she doesn't have any kids to support, but she knew this had nothing to do with Marcia's apparent talent. "Oh how that girl irritates me!"

Her annoyance over Marcia vented itself on her own family. Ordinarily, she very much enjoyed having Jimmy home on summer vacation, but lately he seemed to be a big nuisance. Probably because he was constantly giving Sally a blow by blow description of everything his 'precious Mrs. Evans' was doing. Jimmy liked Marcia too—like father, like son!

Jack was being pushed at the office to complete some work for a new account and had been quite tired and rather irritated each night. Sally hadn't been in the mood to cater to his delicate temperament so she had been snapping at him also.

Jimmy was learning to swim and last year Sally and Jack had installed a swimming pool in their back yard. It was above the ground and the ladder was always removed except when the family was using the pool. Jimmy had strict instructions regarding pool rules and very seldom had to be reminded of safety around, or in the pool. Jimmy was the youngest child on the block and Sally and Jack felt the idea of a pool was a reasonable safe one.

On one hot, sticky August afternoon, Jimmy was in the pool with an inner tube, trying to submerge it, but lacking the weight and strength to achieve this feat. In between failures, he practiced his new skill of diving.

"Look Mom, watch me dive."

A splash of water came cascading over the side of the pool.

"Now watch," he yelled, "I'm going to jump into the tube."

This announcement was followed by another splash.

Sally wished she could be in the pool with him, but knew she had to keep at that mountain of ironing. She had the ironing board in the breezeway, hoping to catch any slight breeze that might flutter past and also keep on eye on Jimmy in the pool.

The telephone rang; Sally was surprised to hear Jack's voice.

"I finished early and it was so hot I thought I'd come home and take a dip in the pool. Can you come to the station and pick me up?"

"O.K. soon as I get Jimmy out of the pool."

She pulled the plug on the iron and called to Jimmy, "C'mon out of the pool, we have to pickup Daddy!"

"Aw, Mom, do I have to go with you?"

Sally thought of the dripping wet bathing suit and the new slipcovers in the car.

"Well, come out of the pool and play in the yard until I get back."

"Okay and he took one more dive into the inner tube.

Sally grabbed the car keys and opened the screen door.

"C'mon now Jim—no fooling!"

As she went toward the car, she heard Jimmy's voice, "Hi, Mrs. Evans."

She glanced toward Marcia's yard and saw her in a pair of blue short shorts and a shapely polo shirt. Hope she's back in her house before I get back with Jack, she said to herself.

The car seat was sticky and hot and Sally felt wilted in the heat. She was greatly annoyed when the car in front of her stalled at the corner and she missed the green light, forcing her to sit another few minutes in the blistering heat. She heard a siren wail, Gee, how I hate that sound, she thought. Wonder who needs the rescuing this time? As she drove up the steaming Main Street she had to pull over to the right to allow the Rescue Ambulance to pass her.

Jack was waiting under the station canopy with his jacket tossed over his shoulder and his tie hanging loosely around his neck. The top button of his shirt was open.

"Boy, is it going to be great to plunge into that pool," he said as he kissed Sally lightly on her nose. "Where's Jim?"

" Oh, he didn't want to come and he was in a wet suit so I told him if he came out of the pool, he could stay in the yard till we got back."

The trip home seemed much longer than the actual eight minutes it took. The heat was stifling. As they turned on to their block, they noticed the red flashing light of the ambulance down the street.

"Jack, that looks like it is in front of Marcia's house— no—oh my God—it's our house! Jimmy!"

As they reached their house, Sally quickly turned off the ignition key and they both scrambled out of the car and pushed their way past a small crowd of their curious neighbors. There was Jimmy, sitting on the grass near the pool, talking with Mr. Dawson, one of the rescue squad workers. Sally rushed over to his side.

"Jimmy—what happened? —Are you hurt?"

"I'm okay Mom—Mrs. Evans saved me!"

"Don't worry, Mrs. Harrison, he's fine now, but if it weren't for your neighbor giving mouth-to-mouth resuscitation, your son wouldn't be here to tell about it. Quick thinker—level-headed, wish she were my neighbor."

Sally looked up to Mr. Dawson's gaze and saw Marcia, standing off from the gathered crowd, her dripping wet shorts forming a small puddle around her feet.

Jack was thanking the rescue workers and listening to Jimmy's version of what happened as Sally walked over in a daze toward Marcia.

"He was telling me about his inner tube as he climbed out of the pool," Marcia said, "and he tripped on the top of the ladder. His head struck the edge of the guardrail and he toppled back into the pool. I called to him, but he didn't answer so I ran over. He was floating in the water face down. I pulled him out—and you know the rest. Mr. Rice passed by the house and I hollered to him to call for help."

Sally stood stunned, staring at Marcia, as tears began to roll down her face. She embraced Marcia and stammered, "Oh—I'm so ashamed, Marcia, after the way I've treated you—you saved his life! Our only child, how can I ever thank you enough?"

"Oh Sally, please, don't embarrass me, --just be my friend. That way, I can enjoy your friendship and your child's too. We'll never have any of our own, and I enjoy children so much."

Wiping her tears and smiling a relieved smile, Sally said, "Come back to our house with me now, Marcia, please, I know Jack will want to thank you and I'm sure Jimmy will too."

"Alright Sally, but first I'd like to change my wet clothes. I'll be over in a few minutes. Then she said, hesitantly, "I'm so glad I was here Sally.'

"You're glad! Marcia, no one could be happier about that, than I am."

Sally started across the lawn to her house. She sure <u>is</u> different, she thought, but there's an awfully <u>nice</u> difference about her.

Big City

"Philadelphia! I've never been out of suburbia before—golly, I don't know whether I like the idea or not yet."

"Well, it's a far cry from Curryville, Sue, but it won't be forever—you'll get used to it."

Tom's job <u>was</u> the important thing----"Okay, Tom, let's take the apartment."

Sue didn't remember anything specific in the marriage vows that said 'Thou shalt live happily ever after in Philadelphia', but it may have been included in that 'better or worse' clause!

The apartment was charming. Built-in dressers and closets with wall to wall carpeting in the bedroom and living room.

"At least we won't have to buy rugs, Tom," Sue said when she saw her new city dwelling. There were three comfortable rooms at a moderate price a month, which the realtor called 'a steal'.

Tom Dolan was working in a brokerage house on Walnut Street, trying hard to build up a clientele, which was no easy task when you were young. Some weeks were much better than others, financially speaking. For this very reason, almost as soon as they were settled, Sue visited the local hospital, which turned out to be Temple University, to apply for a job.

"I prefer to work days in the Emergency Room, Miss Kendal," Sue said eagerly, when she was interviewed.

"At the moment, Mrs. Dolan, we have no openings on days except in the Ear, Nose and Throat Clinic."

Sue cringed inwardly. In her hometown hospital, the field she most disliked was Ear, Nose and Throat. She needed the work, so she agreed to take the offer and start in two days.

130

Sue was to discover that Temple was absolutely nothing like Curryville General.

Early Wednesday morning, Sue bustled around the apartment getting ready for work and fixing Tom's breakfast.

Tom, I've never been on a subway, isn't there any other way I could get to work?"

"When in Rome, honey—and in this section of 'Rome' they subway to work," he said.

Sue was glad to have Tom directing her this morning. Since the subways ran north and south, they had to take a bus first to reach the subway line. They went down some stairs and crowds seemed to form out of nowhere. Everyone was pushing and shoving.

"Excuse me—pardon me," Sue was saying as she tried to keep up with Tom and reach the tollbooth. "I'm sorry, Sir," she said to one man and he stared at her as if she'd lost her mind! " Tom what's the matter with these people!" she gasped when she finally caught up with him. "They act like robots, shoving, pushing, never so much as an 'excuse me for stomping on your foot so hard, lady'. Are they all like this in the city?"

Tom laughed at his innocent country-bred wife. "Only in the subway, where seats and standing space are at a premium," he assured her.

They eventually did get their 'standing space' in the car and were jerked and jostled into motion as it started.

There was much conversation going on, she could hear it above the roar of the motors, yet no one seemed to be actually talking to their neighbor. The car stopped and started half a dozen times and finally Tom said, "O.K. honey, get ready to run"

The door opened and spat out a small crowd onto the waiting platform, then the automatic door slammed again.

Not a sign of a conductor or engineer. How could they know if everyone was clear of the door, she wondered?

Tom was pulling her arm as she gave a final amazed stare at the mechanical monster. He led her up a crowded stairway and into daylight once again.

"There's Temple," Tom was saying, "two blocks up. Think you can find it now?"

Sue was still dazed. "Tom—that subway—"

Tom grinned. "It grows on you Sue. Just remember, there's no such thing as 'ladies first' in a subway. Act like General Grant and charge on to the tollbooth. I'll meet you after work right here. I don't think you're ready to go it alone until tomorrow."

The mere idea of 'alone' made her shudder, but she managed a weak smile and waved as Tom disappeared down those stairs again. Let's see, she thought, did he say left or right? She walked slowly up the street looking up to see if she'd recognize the Temple Clinic, but everything was tall in Philadelphia, and she began to feel like a farmer in the city. She mentally flipped a coin and decided this was the right direction. Two blocks later, she confirmed her choice.

Sue pulled open the door and gave a sigh of relief. Well, at least I'm here—now where do I go, there's fourteen floors! She checked the elevator directory and located her clinic on the seventh floor. A young medical student came to her aid when she reached her floor and stepped out of the elevator looking slightly bewildered. He very obligingly escorted her to the clinic desk. She was to discover that most of the medical students were friendly, and some were too friendly.

She saw an aide standing at the desk. "Good morning, I'm Mrs. Dolan, I'm replacing Mrs. Cooper."

"Oh—yes—you're the one Ms. Kindle told me about, I'm Gladys, look around the clinic for awhile, I'm kinda' busy. I've been runnin' this place alone since Mrs. Cooper left."

She was flabbergasted! An aide telling an R.N. to 'look around because she's busy'! She took a brief turn around the clinic examining rooms to see the layout of the department and gain her composure. Then she came back to the desk where Gladys, 'the chief-in-charge' was bustling around, in and out of the sterilizer room. "I'd like to see this mornings appointments Gladys, please."

"Oh, I'll take care of them today, Mrs. Dolan, I'm used to the patients and the doctors' preferences.

"Yes, I'm sure you are, but I'd like to see them anyway."

Gladys hesitated, then pointed to a brown appointment book and said, "They're in there."

Sue avoided Gladys' gaze and picked up the appointment book, leafing through it until she came to April 14th's page. "Why there's only one name here Gladys, is this the only appointment?"

"Heck, no, we're always filled up—we just don't write them all in the book. We just take care of them as they show up."

"Starting today," Sue said calmly, "all appointments will be listed, Gladys."

"But Mrs. Cooper never did it that way—"

"I'll probably be doing things a little differently than Mrs. Cooper, Gladys, but I'm sure we'll work things out together." Sue knew by Gladys' icy stare, that nothing could be farther than the truth at the moment, but she was an optimist.

That first day was one Sue was not likely to forget in a hurry. At every turn, Gladys bucked her with an excuse for not explaining routine. The doctors seemed to get instruments for themselves rather than ask anyone.

One doctor glanced at Gladys several times, then appeared rather frustrated. Sue asked, "Can I be of some assistance, doctor? I may not be up on the routine but I would like to be of some help."

"Well, thanks, sweetheart," he said with a brighter look on his face, "that's the first free offer of help I've heard in this clinic in some time. I'm Dr. Smith, by the way."

"I'm Mrs. Dolan, doctor."

Sue was able to help more than Dr. Smith had hoped. When they finished with their patient, he asked, "Are you going to be a steady assistant here?"

"Yes, doctor, I just started today."

"Well, let me be one of the first to say welcome. We sure can use some competent nurses—by the way—don't let Gladys buffalo you—let her know she's not indispensable! S he likes to bark, but I've never known her to bite."

Sue smiled, "We'll manage, Dr. Smith."

Throughout the day, Sue offered assistance and introduced herself to the various doctors. Gladys seemed thoroughly irritated. She quickly appeared with supplies when the doctors requested them, before Sue could even begin to find them.

Sue watched closely and said little to Gladys. By early afternoon, Sue felt she could find most of the basic needs without Gladys help, but continued to allow Gladys to produce them.

"See you Thursday at 2 o'clock Mrs. Green," Gladys said to one patient.

"Stop at the desk, please, Mrs. Green," Sue said quickly, "I'll give you an appointment slip."

Gladys bristled!

Sue ignored it and quickly produced a slip of paper for Mrs. Green. Then she wrote her name in the schedule book. She may have missed a few, but by the end of the afternoon, the appointment book was beginning to look important again and Gladys wasn't trying half as hard to hustle the patients out without appointments.

Dr. Clemens, the chief of clinic, asked Sue about various procedures and experimental work he was considering for the clinic and Sue assured him they could work out a schedule to suit his needs. He was very satisfied. "It will mean extra work for a while," he said.

"If it's important to you, doctor, we'll try to fit it in."

"Well, now couldn't ask for much more. Thank you, Mrs. Dolan.

Sue gathered up the soiled instruments and began to clean up the clinic. Gladys had mysteriously disappeared, right after she had eavesdropped on Dr. Clemens' conversation with Sue. As she was sterilizing the last batch, Gladys appeared, trying to be arrogant, but Sue thought she looked a little guilty. "Hi Gladys!" she said sweetly, maybe too much so, she was trying so hard to hide her true feelings. Pretty dirty trick you pulled Miss, but you're not getting me down yet, she thought.

"I have a list of some supplies we'll need. Would you take the requests to the office please? Then I'd like to go over tomorrows' schedule with you."

Gladys looked surprised, but quickly grabbed the list and was gone.

Bet she thought I was going to blow up on her. Well, I even surprised myself, Sue thought. Just scored one for the home team.

Sue sat down at the desk wearily. Guess I'll have all the activity I can handle in this clinic, she said to herself. She began to work out a schedule for the next day, when she suddenly became aware of a shadow near the desk. She looked up to see Gladys standing with two containers of coffee.

"Cream and sugar?" she asked with a grin.

"Yes—thanks,' and Sue couldn't help smiling either.

"Uh –are there any more instruments to clean, Mrs. Dolan?"

"No, they're finished Gladys, but there are some boiling now, you could put them away later if you don't mind."

"Okay--guess we were pretty busy today." You sure do work harder than Mrs. Cooper did."

"You don't do so bad yourself Gladys. Maybe we'll make a pretty good team after all."

Sue met Tom at 4:30 with a smile.

"Guess the 'big city' agrees with you," he said.

"I'm making the adjustment—just watch me take on that subway tonight." And they descended the stairs to meet the 'monster'.

The Carpenter

The day my banker husband became a carpenter was one which I could not possibly forget in a hurry.

We live in a big old white house on a very busy street. Consequently, we do everything to discourage our three children from playing in the front yard. With this thought in mind, my husband and I gave serious thoughts to the building of a playhouse to keep our children occupied in the backyard, and to encourage neighborhood playmates. It was to be a 'just-right' size to share secrets and maybe camp-out.

Bright and early one Saturday morning, Tom started out ambitiously, armed with love, lumber and determination and a set of very unofficial looking dashed-off plans.

"Today's the day, --I'll get the kids to help me, it shouldn't take so long to make."

With optimism like that, nothing I could say would dampen his enthusiasm. I busied myself with my housework, so I could get into the act outside, too. I had hardly started feeding the baby, when—SLAM! The screen-door shut and our five-year-old came running into the kitchen, leaving a trail of early spring mud behind him. "Daddy needs a saw, Mommy," he puffed between breaths.

"Oh he does, huh? Does he think Mommy keeps it here in the kitchen?"

"I don't know—he just said, 'ask Mommy'."

"Okay, pun'kin—sit here and talk to David while I go downstairs and see if I can find it."

A few minutes later, with his treasure in his pudgy hand, he slammed back out the screen-door to the building site.

The baby was almost ready to be plopped into the playpen when the screen-door slammed again. This time it was Susie.

"Daddy wanna' paper 'n pencil, Mommy," she said.

I could see this was going to be a busy morning. I handed the latest helper a pencil and paper and sent her back outside.

"I'm Daddy's helper-girl, Mommy."

"That's right, honey, --bye."

Wondering who would be next, I rushed through the making of beds and right on schedule came a yell from the basement.

"Sal, where's my six-foot rule?"

"Isn't it on your workbench?"

"Don't see it--"came the reply.

I quickly gathered up the clothes for the laundry and went down the stairs to help locate the missing rule. A quick glance over the workbench and the lost was found.

"Thanks," he said with a sheepish grin, and he went out the basement door.

About an hour had passed before I could take a peek at the playhouse, and going to the most logical spot I thought it would be in, a surprise greeted me—it wasn't there! I heard hammer sounds and followed them to the garage. Sure enough, the carpenter and his crew of helpers were busily building a floor, which surprisingly enough, even looked like one.

"Why the garage?" I queried.

"Aw, I don't want the whole neighborhood supervising, I thought I'd get Jack to help me carry it out after it's going better.

"Ryan, go ask Mr. Harris for twelve spikes."

"O.K. Daddy."

"Tell him you want them as long as your hand, with big heads and sharp points."

Ryan looked puzzled at his hand for a moment, but quickly started running on his errand. Mr. Harris owned the hardware store next door.

"Mistah Harris, my daddy wants twelve pipes with big hands like mine and sharp points."

Mr. Harris chuckled—it wasn't the first time the eager errand runner had mixed up a message.

"Let's go see what your daddy needs them for Ryan," he said and they walked out of the store and crossed the wide driveway to the garage.

"Hey Tom, what size pipe do you want?"

"Pipe--I don't want any pipe," then seeing the anxious look on Ryan's face, he grinned and added, "a dozen spikes about so long," indicating with his hands.

"Righto," said Mr. Harris, as he laughed again. No wonder the youngster gets mixed up with an order like that, he thought.

I started back to the house as Tom called, "Bring me something to drink on your next trip out, willya?"

From their kitchen, I heard Susie scream, then crying and by the time I reached the back porch, the tears were streaming down a dirt-smudged face.

"Ohh! —My leg, Mommy, my leg!"

A quick experienced glance assured me it was only a minor calamity.

"Okay, come on in honey, Mommy will fix it with a bandaid."

She sobbed like a tryout for the Academy Award, but after a vigorous encounter with a couple of tissues, the tears stopped and she held the bandaid box while we jabbered about how daddy was coming along with her playhouse. I dabbed gently to clean a chubby skinned-up knee. Once or twice she drew her breath quickly and winced, but soon the first aid was completed and with a big sugar cookie clutched in her tiny hand, she went back to her job as carpenter's helper.

Tom concentrated hard, swinging the hammer, half the time hitting the nails, and occasionally hitting his already blistered thumb, trying hard to create the image that he knew exactly what he was doing!

"Ryan, go get Mommy!"

I was just coming out with a tall iced glass of cherry Koolaid as I heard myself being paged .

"What do you want, Chief?" I asked.

"You're just what I need, --a smart aleck!" He drank the Koolaid quickly. "Thanks. Hold this plywood side up—O.K., now hand me the hammer and those spikes." Then seeing it was humanly impossible to reach all three areas at the same time, while being the main support for a 5x5 sheet of plywood, he said, "Never mind, I'll get them."

I stuck my tongue in my cheek to restrain a retort, but not before he caught a wry grin on my face.

"C'mon now, are you gonna' help or not?—if you're not I'll do it myself. I want to get this done today!"

I realized he was definitely not in the mood for any sarcasm, so I braced myself silently against the would-be wall while he drove one large spike through the plywood into a lonely upright 2x4 on the corner of the flooring. The impact of the hammer rattled my teeth!

"Can you hold that tighter?" he asked.

I never realized plywood had so much bounce to the ounce.

"I'm trying, dear, really!"

Wham! Whack! Bang! I may never have to see my dentist again, I thought.

"Just a few more on the top corner—hold it again."

This time I braced my whole fragile self against the wall and I think I felt my stomach running behind my backbone in sheer cowardice, Wham! Whack! Soon the torture of being a carpenter's helper was over for the moment and both sides of the proposed wall were attached to slightly leaning 2x4's.

"Hand me that level, hon –"

140

I followed orders silently, but when a confused look crossed his face I asked, "How does it look?"

"Oh boy! —You know that bubble that belongs in the middle? —It's not there! Not even on the top or the bottom. If it's <u>that</u> crooked already, I can't make the rest of it square and level or it'll look lopsided."

"I suppose if it's going to lean, it's best to have it all leaning in one direction."

When I received no response to this consoling remark, I thought the best place for me to be was back in the house, so I mumbled something about checking the baby and left quickly.

When evening came, the building had a floor and two walls standing. No frame---no front or back—but two walls standing defiantly! Upon a request for constructive criticism, I refrained from convulsing as I said it looked great—although a little like Perry Winkle's Rinky-Dink Clubhouse. It was a crushing blow to his ego, but with a promise of his very favorite, butter-fried chicken and lemon meringue pie for supper, a very disillusioned, drag-weary carpenter started to pile the tools in Ryan's wagon and decided to call it 'a day of days'.

Many Saturdays have passed since the carpenter's dream first originated, but love and sheer will have won out, and any day in our yard, you may find two of the happiest youngsters enjoying their daddy's handiwork. Even if it <u>is</u> a little off-center and leans a little <u>too</u> much!

The T.V. Patient

Big Mike shuffled deliberately down the long dimly lit corridor. His squinting eyes focused on the familiar bright sign, which read 'Clinic'. He stopped at the doorway and stuck his head in a minute, glanced around the room, looking for his favorite nurse, Miss Shelby—she wasn't there. Another nurse asked, "Can I help you?"

"Miss Shelby comin' in today?"

"Not until later Mike, she had an early appointment—anything wrong?"

"Oh—no—that's all right," he said and shuffled away to the porters closet for his broom.

Mike was almost a fixture at Colby Hospital. He had been a porter there for many years and lived in the dormitories with several of the other male employees who, like Mike, had no other family.

Blonde, petite Miss Shelby, was the one bright spot in Mike's day. He hated to see her days off on the time sheet. He knew they would be lonely ones for him. He leaned his burly frame heavily on his push broom as he lit up his pipe, then stood puffing it awhile, watching other employees going to their departments of work.

"Hi Mike," a heavy-set man said, as he entered the elevator. Then another, "Hi Mike," from a nurse turning another corridor. Mike waved his pipe and gave a nod of his head to them. They were nice enough people but none of them were quite like his Miss Shelby.

He pushed his broom half-heartedly through the basement halls and later pushed wet mops over those same gray tiled floors, glancing frequently at the clinic door. Pretty soon he heard, "Good morning, Mike."

"Hi—Hi Miss Shelby," Mike's face brightened, his double chins shook as he shuffled quickly to the closet where Miss Shelby hung her coat.

"You're looking fine this morning, Mike. Is that a new shirt you're wearing?" She asked.

"Oh—yes-almost new—you like it Miss Shelby?"

"Very handsome indeed! I'll have to keep my eye on you Mike—all the girls will be chasing you."

Mike's ruddy face beamed, she sure had a pretty smile, he thought. She had started across the hall to the clinic room when Mike remembered, "Oh, Miss Shelby, I wonder if you'd get the doctor to look at my chest today—it has kind of a funny sound."

"Sure Mike, as soon as Dr. Jensen comes down, O.K.?"

"Fine thanks."

Mike went back to his work with brightened spirits and a new vigor.

Miss Shelby took a thick brown manila folder from the file. Michael Dombroski – age 56, it read.

"That City Hospital TV show specialized in bronchial asthma last night, Jean," she said to her co-worker, "guess that's what Mike's symptoms will be this morning. Let me warn you, since you're new—never say, 'how are you' to Mike—he'll bend your ear for thirty minutes. It's always much safer to avoid a direct health inquiry.

"I'll remember that," the other nurse laughed.

Sure enough, when Dr. Jensen checked Mikes' complaints a little later, they pointed directly to, 'City Hospital Special Disease of the Week', as Dr. Jensen always described Mikes' maladies. True, he had some minor health disturbances, which included a smokers cough and a healthy appetite for liquor, but on the whole, his health was not too bad.

"Mike I want you to take two of these pills, three times today and tomorrow, and no drinking this week," Dr. Jensen said.

"O.K. Doc—er—ah—not even a little snort before bedtime? It helps me sleep better."

"You heard me, Mike,"

"O.K. Doc—you're the boss—thanks."

"Thanks a lot Miss Shelby, I feel better already," Mike said as he left the clinic.

Several weeks went by, as Mike professed symptoms of Jungle Fever, Mononucleosis, Bursitis of the shoulder, and anything else that 'City Hospital' featured on Monday nights. With each weekly health crisis Miss Shelby was always ready with a kind word for Mike and brief check with the resident doctor.

One morning, as Miss Shelby was reporting for work, she glanced down the corridor expecting to see Mike, but he was nowhere to be seen.

"Hi Jean," she said, as she entered the clinic, "where's Big Mike today?"

"Oh, haven't you heard? —He came in as an emergency last night and was admitted with severe chest pain. He died about 5 a.m.—heart attack, I guess."

"That poor man," Miss Shelby said slowly, "one time that he gets a legitimate complaint and it kills him!"

Slowly she started about her routine duties, feeling an emptiness she hadn't felt before.

"You know Jean, I'm going to Miss Mike, --he was a special guy!"

My First Important Responsibility

I could not decide whether to eat breakfast or not, actually, I was afraid it might be a wasted effort. It was the very first time I would be assigned to a patient. The entire care would be my responsibility. Suppose he was aphasic or incoherent and I could not relate verbally to him or worse yet, suppose he was a good-looking hunk and knew I could blush easily! I finally decided on just toast and coffee and hoped I'd enjoy lunch more.

Mrs. Johnson was a no-nonsense head nurse and I was sure she had no idea how traumatic this day was for me when she briefed me on Mr. Collyer's state of health and the course of care necessary for his maintenance of health. Mr. Collyer had undergone abdominal surgery for cancer and had an abdominal drain in place under massive gauze dressings to absorb any drainage, which turned out to be considerable.

As I approached his bed my knees were shaking so much I was sure he'd hear the knocking from across the room. He smiled back at me as I came closer and greeted him as cheerfully as I could manage. He immediately tried to put me at ease by saying, "Honey, don't you be afraid of me, 'cause I'm sure not afraid of you and I know we're going to get along just fine. You just tell me what you want me to do and I'll try to oblige."

"Maybe you should be just a little afraid of me Mr. Collyer, you are my first exclusive patient. That means I will be doing everything for your care today and I only hope I can do that well and help you to be comfortable."

"O.K. then, I'll be your guinea pig and we'll take it as it comes along."

I could not have been luckier than to have landed Mr. Collyer for my 'guinea pig', he was as friendly as my grandfather.

We managed to cope with a bedbath and dressing change, which bothered me, intestinally speaking, more than it did him. The drainage was odorous and profuse and I'm sure the area was tender to touch even as gently as I handled him, but through it all, he smiled and encouraged my as if I was the most expert nurse he had ever encountered.

It was necessary to change his position in bed frequently to administer injections or to prevent the pressure spots on his tender skin from being irritated and although I didn't know it in the morning, I realized it soon after that each move was saturating his dressings. He never once complained or asked me to apply fresh ones. I soon knew to check them often so I could keep him comfortable and dry.

We were developing a kinship in the days that followed and he seemed eager to talk and have my company present.

Each day was received with a big smile and a cheery hello and even occasionally a joke he remembered to tell me. When I would check his dressings or inquire about his comfort he always assured me he was 'just fine' and not to worry about him, there must be someone else who needs my attention more than he.

By the end of the week we had become comfortable friends and I knew he was being brave, if slightly untruthful, when he told me he was 'just fine'. I told him I would not be there for the weekend because I was going home on my days off and another nurse would care for him while I was away. He said he thought I deserved the days off since I had been so busy all week and he would look forward to seeing me again on Monday morning. I told him I would miss him and not to be 'too hard' on his new nurse. He laughed and promised to be good.

Strangely, Mr. Collyer stayed in my thoughts all weekend, his caring disposition and gentle manner was difficult to forget.

Monday morning early, I rushed to my department to greet Mr. Collyer and was surprised to see his bed empty.

"Where is Mr. Collyer?" I asked Mrs. Johnson.

"Oh he died on Saturday night, had to be taken for emergency surgery and died during the operation. The tumor had ruptured and there was nothing further they could do. You'll be assigned to someone new as soon as I finish my reports."

How could I take care of someone else today! I wanted Mr. Collyer back. I didn't even get to say goodbye to him. What could I have done to have made him more comfortable if I'd been here last weekend? I felt as if I had lost my grandfather, he had been more concerned about my making it through the weekend than himself. There was such an empty spot near my heart, but at the same time a happiness that I had known him, even for a few days. He would always be a special part of my education in caring for people. I knew I would miss him very much.

The Present

It was oppressively hot! Not a clear breath of air to be inhaled. The smog had been sitting on the city like a pot-lid for several days and no encouragement of relief in the immediate future.

The reality of claustrophobia was never so vivid to me before bronchial asthma had returned to my health portfolio.

Repeated trips to the doctor's office offered only temporary relief. The druggist I'm sure was counting his profits every time I brought in another proscription.

Rain was not even threatening the forecast. A heavy shower would surely cleanse the pollen-heavy air.

Fans were running at full speed in every room of the house. Some rooms even boasted two, but still the heat was ever present.

After almost two weeks of furnace weather, a friend arrived at my door with a compact package and a big smile.

"Surprise! Your troubles will be soon over," he said, as he walked past me and marched straight down the hall to my bedroom.

The mystery package contained a small window air-conditioning unit, which he promptly proceeded to install without a word. Within twenty minutes, the magic box sat in my window, happily humming and blowing the most welcome cooled and filtered air into my room. It was just the right size to perfectly cool the room and provide a haven for me to breathe deeply and comfortably.

"Happy Birthday," said my friend.

"But," I protested, "it's not my birthday!"

"Well, you have a much better chance of lasting until it gets here with an early present, so why wait?"

I readily agreed and thanked him profusely, but he shunned my praise and soon was disappearing out the same door he had entered.

Bliss! It's the only word to perfectly describe the change in the air. It was the first step toward recovery.

Several more days passed before the weather conditions changed, but my early birthday present had restored my health and comfort long before the rains came.

The Very Active Summer

Some years it seems days and weeks go by and outside of routine living—nothing special happens! Well, this summer was not one of those times!

It seemed to change tracks in the spring. First there was a death in the family and that meant settling an estate, selling a house, having an auction, dispersing personal momentoes evenly which usually seems to fall on one family while the rest of the family becomes critical of the course being taken.

There was a significant storm that brought strong winds and uprooted a large willow tree in our mobile home park which fell right in the middle of one of the homes during the night.

My husband was out of the country on a trip during this time and called each day to check things at home. That day there was a lot to report! When he asked how everything was going, I told him I had some good news and some bad news. He asked for the good news first and I told him, "He didn't die"! That got his attention. After explaining that the tree had fallen on a tenant's home while he was sleeping, fortunately beyond the area the tree hit, he was very relieved. Local rescue teams had arrived to secure the area and turn off gas and electricity. When they rescued the tenant, he was very calm; a man in his 80's who had lived through storms, an earthquake and many minor mishaps. He was quite deaf and said he hadn't heard a thing. He was quite excited when the prospect of getting a brand-new mobile home was mentioned.

There was major work to be done in our mobile home park, replacing several sewer pipes and preparing a new site for a brand new mobile home which was replacing the destroyed home.   A demo team removed that one.

Backhoes were rented and put to work digging trenches and replacing new sidewalk areas. Then a 14 x 60-foot area was cleaned, leveled, raised above the 100 year flood level and was covered with 11 yards of concrete. No small feat!

During this work time, a new home had to be chosen and ordered, including rugs, wallpaper, room sizes, and appliances. Permits were required, inspections were made of the site, fees were paid and the home was finally ordered. Six weeks later it was driven over the highways to the site we had prepared.

Last minute jockeying into position resulted in minor damage to a wall and some siding which was later repaired by the company. Just a small glitch in comparison.

Now it is two weeks later and it has been 'strapped' to the ground, air conditioner is in place and the electric was just connected. Connections have been made to the water and sewer pipes so there is action in all the pipes and faucets.

Next connection to be made is natural gas and we're 'on their list.'

Outside stairs have been ordered for the emergency exit and skirting is also 'on the way' this week. Appliances are in and most connected except for gas dryer and stove.

Some furniture is drifting in but it won't be approved until the inspectors arrive. That will be the tenant's happiest day. He has been very patient and sitting in his lawn chair daily, watching the show! It has been an adventure in building.

There was no lack of sidewalk supervisors that year. It became the gathering site for tenants toting coffee containers as they commented and added their ideas of how it 'should' be done.

Since the first major 'tree-falling', several large limbs have left their trees and fallen on corners of houses and hot tubs.

. Each 'victim' looks at us hopefully, wondering if it is worth a replacement new home—no such luck! <u>ONE</u> replacement is enough in one summer!

Following the spring, another mobile home was damaged with water—big time! 60,000 gallons worth! Plans are in place to rip out floorboards and insulation and replace with new flooring, plus carpets. Current furniture and appliances was stored until work is done. Hope this completes the major problems in the park this year.

It was an active but interesting venture, but most of the tenants went with the flow and had some activity to observe which provided their entertainment for the summer.

Health Crisis

Some people like to be pampered and waited on, but others would rather be independent, and do for themselves. They never think of being unable to take care of themselves.

I was one of those independent ones until this year when my world crashed in on me suddenly. One day, my legs were a little weak and one week later, I was being transported to the hospital via a 911 ambulance call.

Apparently severe side effects from large doses of prednisone, caused a myriad of serious side effects. A fungal infection in one lung, difficulty breathing, collapsed lung on the other side, leading to a breathing tube and oxygen. Lower back muscles were extremely weak and prevented me from moving freely. Adrenal gland shutdown and various blood test results revealed elevated infection, low hemoglobin, resulting in multiple transfusions. A feeling of severe helplessness overcame me and there was nothing I could do myself to change this. My family was very anxious since they were unaccustomed to my being 'nailed to a bed' in this condition and unable to resist.

After many anxious days in Intensive Care, conditions worsened, internal bleeding resulted in necessary surgery to repair bleeding ulcers, diverticulitis and ruptured blood vessels. Through the course of daily blood testing, my once wonderful veins gave up on me and a direct line was inserted to accommodate further testing and infusions. More transfusions were needed after my blood volume decreased sharply, but when the cause was located and corrected, my health picture improved. After one month in Intensive Care and step-down rooms, I was very weak, but finally well enough to be transferred to a rehabilitation center and spent another month regaining enough strength to return to my home.

Many days were a blur to my memory during this time and many fine and talented doctors and nurses were available and able to treat my unusual problems. My Lord was my main healer and His loving touch along with hundreds of prayers from friends and family was responsible for my eventual healing.

Two months prior to my sudden illness, my husband and I made the decision to be re-baptized, this time by immersion in the Gulf of Mexico, since we were living nearby in Florida. That also was an eventful day since we were 'traveling a little faster' than the speed limit and were signaled over by a local policewoman. We apologized and explained where and why we were going fast but she was doubtful, so we invited her to come and observe the ceremony and she did. She had never viewed an immersion baptism before and was duly impressed. I mentioned to her later that it was probably the most unique excuse she'd heard for speeding and incidentally, she did not give us a ticket!

During the time of my serious illness, I was aware of the severity of my condition but had absolutely no fear about the possibility of dying since I knew I was resting in the arms of my Lord. What a wonderful feeling of peace and comfort I had and know that my Lord had planned all these events for me because He planned to heal and strengthen me in His time while I rested in His arms. How blessed can one be!

The volume of many prayers overcame and triumphed and my health was gradually restored. Many feel it was a miracle, but miracles seem to be something in which the Lord excels. I feel my recovery has been the Lord's choice for me because He has more work He wants me to take part in during my lifetime. I am anxiously waiting to discover this need and willing to pursue the path it leads for completion.

Every life has a purpose. We may not see our path the same as others may see it. Other people and circumstances have a great effect on our viewpoint. Our path often meanders in different directions before we decide on a definite goal. The more fields of endeavor we explore, the more avenues we have to choose. I believe the Lord makes the best choices for us and if we have faith to follow on the path He leads us, we will be fulfilling our life's destiny.

The Therapeutic Pup

Our four-year-old daughter was 'spooked' by motion of small animals and insects, even butterflies. Our two boys were pleading daily for a puppy. The conversation was a constant, "Can we mommy, can we, can we please, mommy?"

Since our daughter was starting school the next year, we had to think of someway to help her overcome her fear. Even walking with her brother on his school path was traumatic to her.

My husband came home one night with the news that our friend, who was a rural dogcatcher, had a female terrier with four puppies. She knew the mother to be very gentle, but did not know who the father was.

We began to consider getting a tiny helpless puppy to solve our problem. Our friend assured us we could return the puppy if it did not work out well. So, one night, just before Christmas, my husband brought home an adorable puppy, complete with fleas and worms!

The boys were thrilled, while our daughter would have been clinging to the chandelier if she could have reached it! The best she could manage was climbing on the back edge of the sofa, clutching her arms together and staring with fearful eyes.

We settled the puppy in a box in the kitchen and provided lots of surrounding newspapers, a small toy and a blanket. Although the boys thought it would be a great idea to take the puppy to bed with them, THAT wasn't going to happen and we explained that the puppy would be going to see the 'dog doctor' tomorrow and be examined to see if it was healthy and get some medicine to treat the worms and fleas.

Later in the evening despite much coaching, we could only convince our daughter to 'peek' at the puppy, as we held her hand.

The next day I took the new puppy to the Vet's office. He was quite amused, since HIS 'puppy' IS A Bull-Mastiff!

He asked all the necessary questions and asked for the puppy's name. I told him, "Donno", and he laughed.

"Where did THAT come from?" he asked.

I told him we knew who the 'mommy' is but we 'donno' who the daddy is.

He eventually pronounced the puppy in good health and gave some shots and pills for her 'problems' and I was soon on my way home with a frisky pup.

Over the coming weeks, the boys had lots of fun playing with 'Donno', and trying to teach her 'tricks' without much success. We bought a leash and a dog sweater so they could walk the puppy outside for exercise and bathroom training.

Our daughter in the meantime was inching her way closer to where the boys were playing with the puppy but if it made a sudden move in her direction she scampered quickly to my side.

One day, while the boys were playing outside, I coaxed our daughter, Susie, over to the puppy while it was lying down and convinced her to pet it tenderly. Since the puppy stayed still, she continued to pet it and seemed to stay calm. I told her how helpless the puppy was and how it depended on each of us to take care of it and love and feed it because she didn't' have a mommy around to do things for her. Susie put some food in a dish and Donno came over to her to sniff and taste it, all the while wagging its' tail.

Each day after, the children took turns giving food and water to Donno.

One morning I came into the kitchen to find Susie playing on the floor with Donno and not seeming to be afraid at all. She seemed to be overcoming her fear at least, about little puppies.

Donno grew rapidly, as most puppies do and became a much-loved member of our family. She seemed to have a strong 'protector' instinct and barked when anyone came to the door. When the children were in bed at night and my husband was attending business meetings, she would position herself right at my feet to be my 'security guard'. The minute my husband came home and sat down in the living room, Donno quietly left me and lay down at his feet. Obviously she saw her job as protecting me until the 'man of the house' came home.

Spring and summer months arrived and Susie was having allergy problems, which needed attention. After visits to the doctor and some allergy tests, we discovered she had developed asthma and apparently an allergy to the dog's dander and fur. Reaching a point where her health was being compromised, we arrived at the decision to give away this dog, and in the future perhaps choose one that did not shed. It was a tearful decision, but we found a family, with a young boy, that lived on a farm and were anxious to give Donno a new home. They even said the children could come and visit in the future which softened the decision to give Donno up to another owner.

Susie had progressed so much since the arrival of Donno, that she happily went off to school in the fall feeling quite brave.

A few years later, we invested in a little white poodle puppy. The doctor felt Susie would have no problem with a non-shedding dog. Once again, every child eagerly tried to teach the new puppy 'tricks' to show off how smart she was. "Mitzi", proved to be a quick learner and was busy every day learning something new.

Mitzi was our much loved permanent pet for more than fourteen years and by then all the children had moved on to college or their own apartments, so Mitzi had served her purpose well in providing love and affection to all of us.

Mitzi developed heart problems that proved to be quite serious and necessitated having to arrange for euthanasia procedures. We didn't want her to suffer and we didn't want her to die when we were away from the house. When arrangements were made, I called Susie and told her what was about to happen and she said she would stop at our house on her lunch hour to say 'goodbye' to Mitzi. Quite naturally, she was upset, but said she would have been more upset if I had NOT called her, which I had considered, to spare her the emotion.

I took the dog to the Vet's office right after lunch and told him I wanted to hold her ' to the end'. Mitzi was calm in my arms since she trusted me, but I began to doubt the wisdom of my decision when I actually felt the life literally 'drop out of her'. Such an emotional moment was more than I anticipated.

We were unable to mention Mitzi's name for many says, due to the emotional loss. Incidentally, since that day, Susie has become involved with a dog rescue organization and her weekends are often kept busy transporting unwanted puppies and older dogs to adoption centers. Her love for animals has come full circle from fear to caring placement.

Now many years later, we've decided not to have another pet. It is too wrenching to have to give them up or lose them to poor health. Instead, we choose to 'borrow' when we feel the need for pet companionship. All of our children have a myriad of pets to choose from when the occasion arises, and then we only have to be concerned with temporary care.

<u>POEMS</u>

That Boy!

He slammed the door
And dropped his book
It made me stop, and turn and look.
The kids all giggled
As he toppled the chair,
He achieved his purpose –
They <u>knew</u> he was there!

He dropped in his chair
And stuck out his feet,
Then rattled the paper
Of a candy treat!
He rifled his desk for a pencil or pen,
To start another day of disruption –again!

If he wanted, he could
Do the work –it was simple;
But he'd rather distract
And grin at me (with that dimple!)

He tried to look tough,
Talked out loud, whistled, teased.
If I raised my voice, lost my 'cool'
He was pleased!

I took up teaching
'cause it challenged my spirit.
Some days, with George, I actually fear it!
But on days when I'm tense
And most nearing despair,
He'll walk in with an apple—
And that grin says, 'I care'.

Helping Hand

Deep in the depths of my despair
I cried out loud—no one was there.
The emptiness filled every inch and square;
So deep was the depth of my despair.

Deep in the depths of my despair
I sat alone, every night and day;
Something had taken my heart away;
So deep was the depth of my despair.

Deep in the depths of my despair
I thought there was no one who'd care;
Who could realize the vacuum there,
So deep was the depth of my despair.

Deep in the depths of my despair
So long alone, I was motionless there.
I could hear the quietness in the air.
Still, deep was the depth of my despair.

One day in the depth of my despair
I heard a voice say, "Of course I care,
Give me your hurt and your despair
And walk with me, I will always be there."

Now, from the depth of my despair,
I've risen up and resumed my cares.
The Lord's at my side, every day, everywhere.
He lifted me out of the depths of despair.

Waisted Action

When fall chills arrived
I found interests inside,
Where it's warm, and cozy and lovin';
So when days often found me
With not much to do
I migrated to my kitchen oven.

Now nothing smells better
Than cookies and cake,
Or homemade bread in the pans;
So I mixed well and stirred,
Folded, beat, punched and spread,
And finished the top with pecans!

With all of these goodies,
One can't just look and sniff—
You <u>must</u> test the product by taste.
So that's just what I did
And when winter is done
I'll find all that good stuff at my waist!

September Pigeons
They've Got My Number

Each year I know
Just when it's September,
'Cause the neighborhood kids
My address will remember.
First, magazines and books
And of course, pleading looks –
Then, cookies and candies galore!
Soon a sponsor for this
A donation for that-
Seems you're setting up camp at the door!
But each young eager face,
So hard to resist-
Is tomorrows' conglomerate force.
Till I learn to say "NO"
To every 'new show'
I'll continue to answer, "Of course!"

Much Ado About Something

In the spring, buds and blossoms appear
And summer brings shade from the leaves;
The beauty of color prevails in the fall
While crops stand high, bunched in sheaves.
The cycle of blossoms and growing then ends,
As the seeds return to the earth.
Winter pulls up a blanket
Says a quiet good-night-
So that spring can expect a rebirth.
Should it be called the 'fall' of the year,
Or 'a covering up' of the ground?
The brilliant colors that were on the trees
Are down at the base in a mound.
Recycling, we thought, was <u>our</u> clever idea;
We must save our planet, we feared.
It's been thought of before- and is working so well-
The Lord makes it happen each year.

Bird Calls

They are mischievous and flighty,
The gift of God Almighty,
But noisy as the devil, just the same.
I admire and I feed them,
Provide, protect and need them
Still when that feeder's empty, I'm to blame!

Do they care about the effort
Or the quality they eat?
Even tho' I know it's summer
And the worms are at their feet!
Still—I love my feathered beauties
And I'll tend to daily duties
As they wait in line to eat there just the same.

The Provider

He visited the feeder
And had his fill of seeds,
Returning to it frequently—
I wondered of his needs.
Perhaps a nest of tiny eggs
Or yet a mate so true,
Depending on his sustenance
To survive the cold days through.
A chirp, a look, was my reward
As daily he'd refuel
And trusted me to fill the bowl
With a daily seed renewal.
Then further into spring, I saw
Another feathered friend.
Familiar features, not so bright,
But daily would attend.
Not so often, would I see
My winter friend arriving.
But equally the two would come
And tend to their surviving.
One day, I looked and pleased my eye
With tiny birds anew,
As timidly they'd peck a seed,
Then fast away they flew.
It seemed the parents honored me
By showing off their brood.
What better place to bring them
Than the new source for their food!

The Busy Season

Spring brings rain and bulbs that sprout
And yard work that needs to be done.
Along with the birds and the buds that burst
Unfortunately, all is not fun.

We cope with the mud and scratch with our rakes;
We trim and edge and seed.
It's been so long, this waiting for spring,
That we work as if filling a need.

We attack with gusto, as we tackle each chore
And bend and stretch and jerk;
It's not till the morrow, the reality dawns,
When those muscles no longer will work.
We vow that next year we'll prepare in advance,
For the work that we do to extreme;
Instead of attacking the first warm spring day
Becoming a chiropractor's dream!

A Gift

It's given to you without any charge
To use just as you please
A brand new day.
What will you do with it?
How will you use it?
Will it be wasted?
Who will control this new day?
Have you made careful plans for it?
It will never be available again.
Will it contain some moments of love,
Moments for sharing or caring
Given with love, no strings attached?
You'll not ever have the same chances again.
So many choices, which will you choose?
Give with your heart, you have nothing to lose.
Maybe your neighbor needs friendship today
Or the neighbor's child just wants you to play;
An errand to run,
Some wild flowers to give,
A smile to a stranger
Some coins to the poor.
The Lord will be watching,
Of that you'll be sure.
Plan carefully how you use your day.

Balance

This world will always need leaders,
But don't the leaders need followers?
There will always be those who are driven by a daytimer,
While others drift through the day
And do only what needs to be done that day.
Some must achieve, or reach a certain goal;
Others stroke the world and help the achievers.
Some are here for recognition,
Others are content with slight notice.
The big movers need their space;
The shufflers fill the nooks and crannies.
Each of us are equally needed,
Though not all for the same purpose.
Some to plan and build the world,
Others to decorate and color it.
Which are you?

What Do You Do All Day, Mom?

What do you do all day, Mom,
Home alone all by yourself,
After the breakfast dishes are done,
And the sugar bowl's back on the shelf?
After the beds are made and fixed
And the laundry's in the machine,
After the papers are all picked up
And the living room's neat and clean;.
After you answer the phone and find
That Jimmy forgot his lunch—
So you throw on a coat and jump in the car,
Rush, don't see the bike—and then CRUNCH!

While you're out in the car
You stop for the 'news'
And notebook paper for Sue,
Then that errand for John,
And another for Dad
And in an hour you're through.
No bread for lunch—
Make it soup—there's the phone
John sprained his ankle in gym!

Pick him up—call the Doc
Pick up bread while you're out
(This must be how she stays so thin.)
Doc can see John at two,
It's too late to eat,
Put your feet up, grab some chicken, (sans skin)
Close your eyes for a sec—
Oh, a withering thought,
The kids must be picked up at three!

What for dinner? Must think—
Thaw it out in the sink
While John's at the Doc's—and x-rays!
Plaster cast in the end—
'Twas a break—not a bend,
And of course, "Keep him home a few days!"

"What do you do all day, Mom?"
Asks Jim, as he comes in from play—
"They want mothers to help in my class.
Teacher asked all the kids
They said their moms have jobs
And I said you do nuthin' all day!"

The Sleeping Giant

A mighty blue spruce, so regal and tall
Being home to the birds near and far,
Uprooted it's feet and fell to the ground
Not a thing in its path did it mar!

It lay in the middle of the yard so still
A darkening mass of green!
The tenants inside, remained where they were
Tho' close to the ground, still unseen.

Hours later, still very confused
One by one, they began to appear
Visiting feeders, all day unused
Thankful, food still remained near.

Many days past 'fore the tree was removed;
By then the storm had passed by.
The tenants, confused, rearranged their lives
Not knowing to stay or to fly.

Weeks went by as they searched for homes
They began to visit for lunch
Fluttering, chirping while gobbling seeds-
We'd both missed each other a bunch!

Edge of Morning

Before the clatter of the day begins—
My world is serene and quiet.
I feel safe and privileged to be able to sit on the sidelines,
On my bugless screened porch and just listen—
As the world awakens, and another glorious day begins.
Full of adventures-surprises-laughter and tears.
I hear water drops as they hit the roof, falling from the trees
Wet from last night's rain
I hear the birds awakening—
Each family calling from their special corner of the woods.
Some chirp, some warble, some give delightful trills of
melody.
While an occasional Jay jabs the air.
The Morse code of nature sends its signal to the world
All is well, morning is here, life goes on.
The squirrels scamper from tree to tree making branches
swish and twigs snap.
As they chase their way to breakfast.
No horns or screeching brakes, no bells or shouting voices.
Just the tranquil sounds of morning.
An airplane rumbles overhead to its' destination,
Sometimes making vacuum sounds as it sweeps the sky.
My resident groundhog silently sneaks up on my flower
garden.
'Looking for a stolen treat-perhaps another dahlia bulb!
A dull thump at my front door signals the arrival of the
daily newspaper.
One of the many "early people" that start my day.
The day-lilies are still snoozing.
Waiting for the wake-up message to open their petals.
The pansies are already spilling their splashes of color over
the side of their containers.
The quietness of God is awesome!

The sun is lightening the world, but the clouds filter its' normal brightness
As the drizzles and dew drops finish their work.
There are no blaring radios or urgent, catastrophe of the day, T V reports.
The world is at rest and all is well.
Wet footprints scatter my lawn from early breakfast seekers.
An occasional worm is being yanked from its' bed.
No garbage trucks with their cacophonic beeping back-up sounds.
The morning begins with vigor.
More sounds of planes, traveling their paths
To start other days in distant places.
A woodpecker noisily starts his day;
The local train gives its' distant whistle to jostle the commuters into action.
Traveler cups of coffee in hand, Newspapers tucked under their arms
And briefcases in hand, as they begin their journey to the hectic world of business.
In a short while, I'll hear an urgent staccato ringing of my doorbell,
Followed by an anxious call- "Grandma, where are you? I'm here!"

Change of Heart

"I think I should stay home today—I'm sick!"
"Tell the nurse! Be on your way!"
Not ready for test in English Lit –
Oh—how can I get out of it?
Think I'll wait till period three
Then I'll get excused to the nurse, and see
If I can lie down with a 'stomachache'
(Hope she won't guess it's just a fake!)
Should have studied for it last night
But wanted to see the heavyweights fight.
If I don't get a decent grade
My folks will have a great tirade!
Oh why didn't I take notes in class-
Have to do something or I won't pass.
If only I had to do over again
I'd do things diff'rent
'Cause this is PAIN!
I'd love to be on an honor roll
Though I know it takes lots of work.
Still I envy the kids that make it,
And I used to think they were jerks.
Well, I've five weeks left
And enough time to spare.
I'll buckle right down,
Soon they'll know I do care.
My parents would flip
If my average I'd change;
They must feel that college
Is out of my range.
They'll think it unusual when good grades appear
But they'll like it- with graduation so near.
They'll start saying stuff-like "He takes after me."
And "You mark my words, a doctor he'll be!"

You know, it's funny
They prob'ly knew I could do it.
If I hadn't waked up, I just might have 'blew it'.

My Teddy Bear

My teddy bear, my teddy bear,
He meant so much to me
He heard me laugh and felt my tears
He was as real as real could be.
His coat was brown and curly
His eyes were bright as stars.
He stayed with me thru thick and thin
He even bore some scars.
I could lie my head upon him
And tell him all my fears;
I could wrap my arms around him
Feeling safe with him so near.
My friend and I made clothes for him,
Striped pants and 'spenders ' blue,
He looked so kingly then to me
With a coat and vest so new.
He wore no shoes
'Cause he was a bear-
Just a jaunty cap
On his curly hair.
He was my friend forever there
And he went with me everywhere
So many memories we could share,
If I still had my teddy bear.

My World Through Her Eyes

The crisp air whispered in the night,
The moon glowed in the sky;
Who knew before the morning light
My dearest friend would die.

She'd been with me for many years,
No better friend than she.
She understood and shared my dreams
And gave of her love to me.

We walked together, she and I
Not needing to make a sound,
I'd pat her head and brush her fur
When no one was around.

Without my having to say a word
She'd guide each step safely;
Who ever knew tomorrow
She'd no longer be with me.

She left me silently in the night;
As I quietly slept nearby;
Someone else guides my steps today,
My dearest friend has died.

Uncrossable Chasm

Are you doing your share?
Are you doing enough?
Do you show that you care,
When the going is rough?
Is there more you can do?
Is there time for a prayer?
When you're down at the bottom.
Is there love you can share?
A soft word of comfort,
A strong helping hand.
Words of encouragement,
An unpopular stand?
There is much to be gained
If you do this today,
Because once you are gone
The chance is taken away.
From across the chasm
In death, there's no changing,
W hat could have been done
Is past re-arranging.
When the poor and the needy
Are comforted with care,
You'll be past the chasm,
With no kindnesses there.
When selfishness keeps you
From giving love and care,
Just remember, do it right now,'
Since you can't do it from there.

Where is God?

I know He is there,
All around, in the air
But I can't see Him;

I know He is there,
In the flowers and trees,
But I can't touch Him.

I know He sees me
And all that I do,
If I'm good or I'm not,
He still will love me.

He gave me the world,
For this world He has wept.
If I love only Him
In His arms I'll be kept.

What more could I ask?
What more could He give?
He gave His whole life for me.

The Church

It beckoned to me in the night
As a light sends a shaft—like a path.
It said, "I am the Light of the world."
And an overwhelming force drew me to the source.
I felt a welcome healing from those who greeted me
And if I was not present, I was actually missed.
The true concern for my physical and emotional feelings
was sincere;
Saying, let us show you what is available to you
And how we can help you achieve it.
I knocked, and the door was opened to me;
I sought the light, and it lead me;
I asked, and all I needed was given to me.
Love cannot contain more than this—
My heavenly Father enveloped my life.

The Chimney Guard

He stands a mighty fixture
On my chimney, seeing all;
And every day, so loyal
Like a guardian standing tall.
Though winds may blow
This sentry is ever at his post,
With his quiet silent presence
Though he's overlooked by most.
When walking through your neighborhood
Observe and see him there—
Looking, watching, ever vigil
Never taking to the air.
Such friendship, true and faithful
Is mighty hard to sever
But my trusty iron owl
I know will leave me never.

Winter Storm

With not a sound of warning
So silently in the night,
Blanketing the earth below
It covered everything in sight.

The gusty winds whipped constantly
Hours passed, it continued to fall.
Nothing spoiled the cover of white
Not a car or person at all.

Monstrous drifts were building
Icy sleet and hail and snow.
All thru the day and into the night
The wind continued to blow.

When came at last the morning,
It sat silently on the ground;
And soon an army of shovels
Moved it noisily all around.

The Saga of Hackettstown's Golden Skillet

Out in the country where the river flows by,
Is a busy little kitchen where the chicken does fly.
It's called Golden Skillet, and it serves the best-
The happy people there serve the smiles and the rest.
Every now and then, the suppliers do change
And problems do arise of a varied and sundry range.
It seems we have a problem, or two or three or more—
But we're confident that Southland will solve them all for sure!
First it was the peanut oil
That simply cost too much;
So we talked to Betty about it—
She said the market was up and such;
Then the trash bags didn't fit at all!
So Betty once more gave her special touch
And again Southland stood tall.
So we tip our hats to Southland
And we threw in a round of applause
Because anyone who makes our day easier
Is truly our Santa Claus.

About the Author

Nancy Budd has had a varied career, which includes: Registered nurse, wife, mother, restaurateur and volunteer. She has culled some of her writings from these experiences.

Some of her essays have been published and well received in her hometown newspaper, The Gazette, in Hackettstown, N.J.

This is her first venture gathering her writings in a book. Originally intended for friends and family, she hopes you will also enjoy reading her collection of human interest and sometimes-inspirational essays, short stories and poems.

Nancy currently is living in Florida with her husband, where they are enjoying retirement near some of their family members and grandchildren.